In this beautifully written and acce_ ....
leads his readers through the Buddhist ways of reflecting and
contemplating. Addressing the sources of our suffering arising
from our short lives here, full of anecdotes and wisdom from
personal experience, this is a gem of a book that can be savoured
and will enlighten.

Professor Paul Gilbert,
author of *The Compassionate Mind*

Reflection is an important element in the spiritual life, and
Ratnaguna explains what it is and how it is to be cultivated.
He also shows how reflection connects with other aspects of
the spiritual life, especially meditation. The book is based on
personal experience, and Ratnaguna writes from the heart,
though the book is also the product of a keen and searching
mind. The six chapters are enlivened with a variety of apt
quotations, both scriptural and literary. No one who takes
seriously the study and practice of the Dharma should fail to
read this ground-breaking book.

Urgyen Sangharakshita,
founder of the Triratna Buddhist Community

The Art of Reflection will give teachers insight into Buddhist
practice. Even more importantly, it may help to develop the
ability to engage in deeper personal and professional reflection.

Joyce Miller,
REtoday

Whoever wants to establish an effective reflection practice will
find useful support in this book. The clarity, love and empathy
with which this book has been written, show the longstanding
practice and experience of the author. The author opens a
unique, fresh and unprecedented perspective on the art of
reflection, an art which promises wisdom through thinking.

Andreas Hubig,
Buddhismus Aktuell

The Art of Reflection

A Guide to Thinking,
Contemplation and Insight
on the Buddhist Path

Ratnaguna
(Gary Hennessey)

W indhorse Publications

Published by
Windhorse Publications
169 Mill Road
Cambridge
CB1 3AN
UK

info@windhorsepublications.com
windhorsepublications.com

First edition 2010
New edition 2018

Printed by Bell & Bain Ltd, Glasgow

Cover design by Dhammarati
Cover image Paul Cézanne, *Portrait of the Artist's Son*, 1885

British Library Cataloguing in Publication Data:
A catalogue record for this book is available from
the British Library.

ISBN: 9781 909314 97 9

Dedication

....

For Scheherazade

About the author

Ratnaguna was ordained into the Triratna Buddhist Order in 1976, and he now teaches and trains others to teach Buddhism.

He is also the author, with Śraddhāpa, of *Great Faith, Great Wisdom – practice and awakening in the Pure Land sutras of Mahayana Buddhism*, and *The Little Mindfulness Workbook* under his civil name Gary Hennessey.

Acknowledgements

Many, many thanks to my teacher, Urgyen Sangharakshita, who taught me by example how to think critically and creatively. Thanks also to all the people who have attended my reflection workshops and helped me to understand better what reflection is and how to do it. Much gratitude to all the writers who have inspired me to reflect more deeply, especially those I have quoted in this book. Thanks to my editor Vidyadevi, who skilfully pointed out ways in which my book could be improved, and graciously accepted my occasional unwillingness to change something. Thanks also to my friend Nagapriya who gave me invaluable feedback when he read the second chapter. Perhaps the book would have been better if I'd made all the changes that he and Vidyadevi suggested. I can be stubborn though. Finally, huge gratitude to the Buddha, that greatest of reflective thinkers.

Contents

Introduction

First there is a mountain then there is no mountain then there is.

Donovan

This is a book about reflection as a spiritual practice. Reflection comes from the Latin *reflectere*, which is made up of two parts: *re*, meaning 'back', and *flectere*, 'to bend, curve or bow'. *Reflectere* therefore means bend back, turn back, or turn round. A reflection on the surface of a lake or a mirror is the effect of light being turned back from that surface, and when we reflect, our thoughts turn back, or turn around, on a subject. To reflect, then, means to think about something, although it's a certain kind of thinking. While we're awake we're thinking most of the time – that is, thoughts are going through our head – but we're not always reflecting. Reflective thought takes practice and discipline. It's an art. The dictionary tells me that in this context art consists in 'the principles or methods governing any craft or branch of learning: the art of baking; the art of selling'.[1] I like those two down-to-earth examples. Just as you can learn how to bake or sell, or become better at baking or selling, you can also learn how to reflect, or become better at it than you are now.

In the repertoire of Buddhist practices that are available to us, reflection is one of the most neglected by contemporary writers on Buddhist practice. In fact, reading some books, you'd think that Buddhists aren't supposed to think at all, as if thinking somehow contaminates the mind. Of course, if we're honest, we have to admit that a lot of what we think about *does* contaminate our minds, but that doesn't mean that *all* thinking is bad. Someone who eats only junk food will become ill, but they shouldn't stop eating altogether; they need to eat nutritious food, and similarly, we shouldn't stop thinking, we just need to be careful what we think and how we think about it. It's also possible to think too much, to over-conceptualize, to be 'too much in our head' as we say, and when we do that we lose touch with our actual lived experience. The remedy for this is not to stop thinking altogether, but to learn to think more consciously and when it's appropriate.

Thinking of any kind is discouraged by some writers and teachers, probably because they consider meditation to be *the* most important Buddhist practice – and thinking is a distraction when you're trying to meditate. But again, that doesn't mean that thinking is in itself a bad thing, it just means that thinking and meditating don't go together very well – they are different practices, to be done at different times. We know from our experience that there are many activities that don't go very well together: reading a book and having a conversation; cooking a meal and re-potting your plants; making love and answering the phone. None of these activities is inherently bad, but it's better not to do them simultaneously. It's the same with thinking and meditating.

At the time of writing this book, some Western Buddhist teachers and writers are tending to place a strong emphasis on awareness of the body. I'm sure that this is a good and necessary corrective for many Westerners, susceptible as we are to the tendency to think too much and 'live in our heads'. We need to include the whole of ourselves in our practice, including our bodies. However, some of the advocates of body awareness go to the other extreme and suggest that thinking is somehow unspiritual, incompatible with treading the Buddhist path. But we have a brain and we need to take that with us too! Enlightenment is a state of wholeness which includes the body, heart *and* mind, and we won't achieve wholeness by denying any part of ourselves.

This book then is unashamedly about thinking, considering, pondering, wondering, cogitating, reasoning, imagining, contemplating – in a word reflecting – within the context of Buddhist practice. I've tried to show how important reflection is if you want to understand yourself, other people, and the world at large better, and how that understanding can go some way to alleviating your own and other people's suffering. I've also tried to show how enjoyable reflection can be, as well as (sometimes) challenging, and how you need to bring the whole of yourself into reflection so that it's not merely a mental exercise. I've suggested a number of different ways to reflect, and how to develop and deepen your reflections; and I've tried to encourage you to take yourself seriously as a practitioner of reflection. While this book isn't exactly a workbook, with exercises etc., it *is* primarily a practical manual. It's a 'how to' book. Before we plunge into the practicalities though, I want to situate reflection within the Buddhist tradition. If you're not particularly interested in that, you can skip the next bit and go straight onto the section headed 'Dimensions of Reflection' on page 19.

The Buddha and reason

The Buddha was actually a great thinker, and he valued reason very highly. There is a record in the early Buddhist texts of a conversation between the Buddha and the follower of another spiritual tradition, in which they disagreed on a fundamental point of doctrine. The Buddha said: 'If you will debate on the basis of truth, we might have some conversation about this.' A little later, when his interlocutor had contradicted himself, the Buddha warned him to 'pay attention how you reply! What you said before does not agree with what you said afterwards, nor does what you said afterwards agree with what you said before.'[2]

Not that the Buddha valued reason above all else. He wasn't a rationalist philosopher; his insights into the nature of reality went 'beyond the sphere of reason' as he put it, but he was never *irrational*. Some people think that when the Buddha said that his wisdom was beyond the sphere of reason, what he meant was that he had left reason behind – discarded because of no value. However, the word 'beyond' can be understood in two different ways: we can go beyond something in the sense that we leave it behind, or in the sense that we include *more than* that something, while continuing to include it.

Let's say that one day, while walking in the countryside, you get lost, and you ask a local farmer for directions to a certain village. He tells you to 'go beyond the wood, and you will come to the village'. Beyond in this sense means leaving the wood behind to reach the village. Let's imagine now that this farmer is gregarious and that he engages you in conversation. At one point in the conversation you ask him how far his land extends, and he replies: 'You see the road down in the valley? My land extends beyond that as far as the tree line at the top of next hill.' Beyond in this sense means further than, but *including*, the road in the valley. The Buddha's wisdom is beyond the sphere of reason in this second sense: it is greater than anything reason is able to reach or describe, but it doesn't leave reason behind.

Well, it may leave it behind temporarily. Let's imagine that you have your conversation with the farmer while standing in one of his fields. It's a large field, and he tells you that it used to be much smaller. The easternmost fence used to run on this side of the oak tree, but a few years ago he decided to enlarge the field, and the new fence lies beyond the oak tree. The field used not to include the oak tree, but now it does. Let's imagine the farmer putting up the new fence on the other side of the oak tree. While he's doing this, he is not simultaneously standing in what used to be the old, smaller field. He has had to leave the smaller field behind in order to enlarge it. Once he has finished putting up the new fence though, he takes a walk around the whole field to get a sense of its new dimensions. The old small field is now included in the new large field. In a similar way, when the Buddha experienced direct insight he was probably not thinking very much, if at all. So we could say that at such times he did in fact leave reason behind. His insight was non-rational, or supra-rational. But later he reflected on his insight and put it into words. When he did that his insight *included* reason, even though it was beyond reason, in the sense that there was more to the Buddha's insight than reason could fully describe.

The distinction I've just made between beyond as 'leaving behind' and as 'more than but including' is important because if you think that the Buddha's wisdom is beyond reason in the first sense, it's easy to conclude that reason is of no value, even that it's a hindrance to the spiritual life. After all, if you want to get to the village it's important that you *do* leave the wood behind, otherwise you'll be stuck in the wood forever and never reach your destination! Some Buddhists

The Art of Reflection

seem to consider reason to be like the wood: something to be left behind, like greed and hatred. This attitude is often accompanied by an over-valuation of faith and intuition, which leads, in turn, to a dogmatism which makes discussion difficult if not impossible. Someone who regards reason as unimportant might say 'I can't explain it, I just *know* it's true', but if they can't explain it to others, do they really understand it themselves? I'm not suggesting that faith and intuition are not to be trusted at all – in Chapters 4 and 5 I argue that they are valid forms of knowledge – just that we can't rely on them absolutely. The Buddha once said that 'something may be fully accepted out of faith, yet it may be empty, hollow and false; yet something else may not be fully accepted out of faith, yet it may be factual, true and unmistaken.' Therefore, he said, faith doesn't give us adequate grounds for coming to a definite conclusion that 'only this is true, anything else is wrong.'[3]

The difference between beyond in the sense of 'leaving behind' and in the sense of 'more than but including' can be simply illustrated in two diagrams:

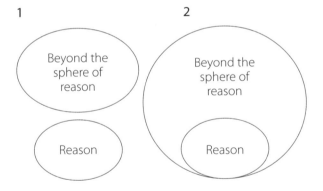

As you can see, if the Buddha's wisdom had left reason behind, as in diagram 1, there would be no connection between them, which would mean that he would have been unable to teach what he had learned through direct insight. The second diagram shows that, although the Buddha's insight was greater than reason, they are still connected – there is a relationship between them. We'll explore that relationship in Chapters 1 and 6.

The Three Levels of Wisdom

There is a teaching which includes reflection as a necessary stage of the Buddhist path, called the Three Wisdoms or Three Levels of Wisdom. They are: 1) Wisdom through (or by means of) Listening; 2) Wisdom through Reflecting; and 3) Wisdom through Contemplating. The first level, Wisdom through Listening, is so called because the Buddha never wrote his teachings down – he only taught verbally. The Buddha's immediate disciples in fact were called *sāvakas*, which means 'listeners'. For the first few hundred years of its existence Buddhism was an oral tradition: teachings were passed on by word of mouth, so listening was the only way of learning from others. This level of wisdom then represents learning from the wise, and these days it includes reading as well as listening.

The second level of wisdom is gained through reflecting. Once you have heard (or read) a teaching you then need to think about it. Talking of the ideal disciple, the Buddha once said :'Having heard the Dhamma (i.e. the Buddha's teaching), he memorizes it and examines the meaning of the teachings he has memorized; when he examines their meaning, he gains a reflective acceptance of those teachings.'[4] Obviously if you don't have access to the written word, so that listening is your only way of learning teachings, it's important to remember what you've heard, otherwise you can't really examine it. Reading allows us to examine the meaning of a written text without having to memorize it. Clearly there are advantages to being able to read texts, but there is an advantage to memorizing teachings too: it allows us to reflect on a teaching at any time, in any situation, without the need for a written text.

When you think about something you've learned, you go deeper into the meaning. You see implications that you may not have noticed on first hearing. You may also encounter problems, things that you don't fully understand or that seem to contradict other teachings, and you have to work out the solutions for yourself. Or you may question something – 'Is this really true?' Or you may think about how the teaching might apply to you, and in this way you 'translate' what may be a general and theoretical

The Art of Reflection

teaching into something more specific and practical. As a result of reflecting in this way you come to a deeper understanding of the teachings than you did when you first heard them, and this deeper understanding the Buddha called a 'reflective acceptance'. You now accept the teachings, not out of faith – not because they have come from the Buddha and therefore they *must* be true, or because you think that you *should* believe them – but because after careful examination you can see that they make sense.

It's important to understand that reaching a reflective acceptance of a teaching is not the same as having direct insight into it. It means that, after giving it serious consideration, you are now intellectually convinced. That conviction is not a guarantee that the teaching is true, or that you have fully understood it. I quoted the Buddha above, telling us that having faith in something doesn't mean that we can be certain that it's true, but he said the same about reason: 'Something may be well reflected upon, yet it may be empty, hollow and false; yet something else may not be well reflected on, yet it may be factual, true and unmistaken.' Therefore, he said, reflection doesn't give us adequate grounds for coming to a definite conclusion that 'only this is true, anything else is wrong.'[5] Insight *is* beyond – in the sense of greater than – the sphere of reason.

The third level – Wisdom through Contemplating – is the practice of meditating on a teaching. It differs from reflecting in that when you contemplate you don't *think* about a teaching, you simply hold it in your mind and allow it to percolate through the whole of your being. At this stage we try to go beyond the sphere of reason, in that we try to have a direct experience of the way things are, unmediated by concepts. This experience is often known by Buddhists as *insight*, which is a translation of the Pali term *vipassanā*. I discuss contemplation and insight in more detail in the second half of the fifth and the whole of the sixth chapter.

Progressing through the three levels

An ancient Indian school of Buddhism called the Sarvāstivāda gave a memorable simile that describes the process of moving though the three levels. Imagine that you are standing on this side of a very wide river, wanting to get to the other side. There is no bridge and you can't swim, so how are you going to get across? If you know anything about Buddhism you'll probably recognize this image. This side of the river represents ignorance, while the further shore is Enlightenment. You'll probably also be familiar with the standard way to cross over – you need to gather some logs and tie them together to make a raft, and then use this raft to ferry you across to the other side. The raft is the Dharma; the teachings and practices the Buddha taught. Once you've made it to the other side, you step off the raft onto the shore. You don't need it any more – the Dharma is a means to an end, not an end in itself, and once you're Enlightened you no longer need it.

Crossing the river on a raft is one of the most famous metaphors in Buddhist literature and teaching, but the Sarvāstivādins (the followers of the Sarvāstivāda school) suggest another way of crossing: they say you need some 'swimming apparatus'. Considering that this school existed in India some 2,000 years ago, the swimming apparatus won't consist of a rubber ring or a pair of armbands. It will be something much more basic – something like a log. So, you find yourself a log, you throw it into the water, and you hang on to it, kicking with your legs. Remember, you can't swim, so you'll be hanging on to that log for dear life. However, as you move slowly towards the other shore you begin to feel a little more confident in the water, so you let go of the log for a moment to see what happens. That's a bit scary, and you take some water into your mouth, so you grab hold of the log once again. After a while though, you try letting go of the log once again, and this time it's a bit easier – you're gaining confidence. However, you still can't swim and so you catch hold of the log again. This goes on for some time – hanging on to the log – letting go – hanging on – letting go – all the time getting closer to the other shore. Then there comes a time when you let go of the log and realize that you don't have to go back to it – you can now swim – so you can now make your own way, leaving the log behind *before* you have quite reached the other side.[6]

In this simile, hanging on to the log represents Wisdom through Listening. When you start practising the Dharma you need to 'hang on' to the teachings of those who are wiser than you. You *need* their wisdom. Alternately letting go of the log and then going back to it represents Wisdom through Reflecting. Thinking requires a certain amount of independence: you need to have the freedom to entertain the possibility that the teachings you're considering may not be true. If you don't have that kind of freedom then you're not really thinking. So you have to 'let go' of the teachings in order to think about them, but you also have to keep returning to them because you are still a learner – you haven't yet had a direct insight into the way things are, so you still need to rely on those who have. Letting go of the log and swimming the rest of the way represents Wisdom through Contemplating. Now you can swim so you no longer need any assistance from outside yourself – you no longer need others to tell you how things are. At this point you become what the Buddha called 'independent in the Dharma'.

Do we leave previous levels behind?

This simile suggests that as we progress through the levels of wisdom we go beyond the previous level in the sense that we leave it behind. In a way we do, and in a way we don't. We have to remember that similes have their limitations, and while 'letting go of the log' describes one aspect of the process, it doesn't do justice to another. One way of understanding the progress through the three levels is as a movement from reliance on external authority to reliance on internal authority. When we practise the first wisdom – listening – we rely on the wisdom of others (we hold onto the log). The result of practising the third wisdom – contemplation – is reliance on our own wisdom (we let go of the log and swim). The second wisdom – reflection – represents the midway point in that movement (we alternately let go of and catch hold of the log). Understood from a modern, Western perspective this might mean that when you reach the third stage you have gone beyond the teachings, in the sense that you have left them behind, and you now have your own unique wisdom – 'your own truth', in the common phrase. However, we need to be careful to try to understand what this progression means from a Buddhist perspective. When you reach the third stage you have had an insight into what your teachers and texts have been trying to describe. It's not 'your' wisdom. You've simply seen what others before you have seen. What you've gone beyond is not their teaching but your own previous merely rational understanding of that teaching.

This difference of interpretation is important. Modern Western society places a high value on the notion of 'thinking for oneself', the goal of which is to have one's own original thoughts on everything. This is not the aim of Buddhist reflection, which is to see things as they are. Others have seen things as they are before us, so any insights we may have will not be original. We may express them in an original way, and of course we live in a very different society to those in which the ancient sages lived, so we'll have new, perhaps original things to say about our society, but originality of thought is not the aim of Buddhist reflection. Depth of wisdom is what we're after.

The Sarvāstivādins, who gave us the simile of the swimming apparatus, taught that reflection functions as an intermediary between the first and third levels of wisdom. In this context they call the first level 'the word' and the third level 'the experience' – experience, because here they mean not the *practice* of contemplation but the *experience* of direct insight brought about by contemplation. They ask a question: how do you get from the word to the experience? That is, how do you transform the teachings you have learned into direct insight? The answer is: by means of the second level – by reflecting on those teachings. They then ask another question: how do you get from the experience to the word? Now you may wonder why that would be necessary. There are a number of reasons, but I'll mention just one here. When you have an experience that you interpret as insight, how do you know it's genuine? You need to check it against the teachings, and you do that by means of reflection. So there is a two-way movement between listening and reflecting, as there is between reflecting and contemplating:

Listening←→Reflecting←→Contemplating

Dimensions of reflection

I hope it's clear from what I've written how important reflection is in the living of the spiritual life. However, I can't remember ever reading a text that explains *how to do it.*[7] We're left to our own devices. That seems an important omission doesn't it? Perhaps the sages of old thought that it wasn't necessary to explain – perhaps they thought it was obvious. And no doubt there are people who just get on with it and don't need any help – natural reflectors! However, in my experience of teaching Buddhism over the last thirty years, I've noticed that people are attracted by the idea of reflection, and they want to reflect more than they do, but they often need some guidance and encouragement. That's why I've written this book, and as I haven't come across any Buddhist texts to help us I've drawn on my own experience, with a little help from a few Western writers from the fields of philosophy, literature and psychology.

Until now I've been discussing reflection very specifically as the reasoned examination of Buddhist teachings, but there is more to it than this. It has many dimensions and levels, which we'll be exploring in the following chapters. D. H. Lawrence touches upon some of these dimensions in his poem *Thought*:

> Thought, I love thought.
> But not the jiggling and twisting of already existent ideas
> I despise that self-important game.
> Thought is the welling up of unknown life into
> consciousness,
> Thought is the testing of statements on the touchstone of
> the conscience,
> Thought is gazing on to the face of life, and reading what
> can be read,
> Thought is pondering over experience, and coming to a
> conclusion.
> Thought is not a trick, or an exercise, or a set of dodges,
> Thought is a man in his wholeness wholly attending.

Lawrence writes that 'thought is not the jiggling and twisting of already existent ideas', and that it 'is not a trick, or an exercise, or a set of dodges'. It's not merely an intellectual game. His conception of thought is in fact very close to what I mean by reflection, and in Chapter 1, 'A Reflective Life', I discuss the importance of referring our thinking to our experience. Not that we shouldn't think about ideas, but those ideas should refer as closely as possible to real life.

So what *is* the kind of thought that Lawrence loved (and, incidentally, that I love)? It is 'pondering over experience, and coming to a conclusion.' To ponder is 'to consider something deeply and thoroughly',[8] and Chapter 2, 'Learning from Experience', is about this kind of reflection. Someone told me that they once asked our teacher, Sangharakshita, how they might become wise, and he apparently answered: 'Reflect on everything that happens to you.' If we add to that 'everything that you do', that just about covers everything, doesn't it? Don't expect to come to conclusions immediately though. Sometimes you might ponder on your experience for a long time before coming to any kind of conclusion. Another poet, Rainer Maria Rilke, wrote:

> Have patience with everything unresolved in your
> heart and try to love *the questions themselves* as if they
> were locked rooms or books written in a very foreign
> language. Don't search for the answers, which could not
> be given you now, because you would not be able to
> live them. And the point is, to live everything. *Live* the
> questions now. Perhaps, then, far in the future, you will
> gradually, without even noticing it, live your way into
> the answer.[9]

Thought is gazing on to the face of life, and reading what can be read. When we reflect we try to see what is there, right in front of us. The Zen teacher Dogen wrote, about reflecting on impermanence: 'It is not creating something out of nothing and then thinking about it. Impermanence is a fact before our eyes.'[10] Reflection is *disinterested* thought. This doesn't mean *uninterested*, it means unbiased by personal interest or advantage. When we reflect, what we're interested in is discovering the truth, even if the truth is uncomfortable or inconvenient to us. I discuss this at some length in Chapter 2.

Thought is the testing of statements on the touchstone of the conscience. A touchstone is a hard black stone, such as jasper or basalt, formerly used to test the purity of gold or silver by comparing the streak left on the stone by one of these metals with that left by a standard alloy. Conscience is our inner sense of right and wrong (or as Buddhists put it, skilful and unskilful). Lawrence says that one of the functions of thought is to test statements or ideas against our inner sense of what is right or wrong – skilful or unskilful. Reflection has an ethical dimension. He doesn't specify whether the statements that we should test are our own or someone else's, so let's assume that he means both. In the case of other people's statements, we've already seen that reflection includes the testing of teachings against reason and experience, but there is also a sense in which we should test ourselves. We shouldn't only examine the teachings; we should also examine our conscience against those teachings. When we hear or read something that comes from a source that we trust, and that seems true, *we* are called into question. If we reflect, for instance, on the Buddha's statement: 'Hatred never ceases by hatred. Hatred only ceases by love', we might first ask ourselves if the statement is true, in all cases. If we come to the conclusion that it *is* true, then the next thing to do is reflect on where we stand in relation to that teaching. Are we friendly to those who hate us, or do we retaliate with hatred? We'll be exploring this area in Chapter 4, 'Reading Reflectively'.

Then there are the statements that we make. Are they true? How do we know? If true, do we live by them? The Pali word *sati*, which is usually translated as 'mindfulness', also means conscience, and writing this book has been a real education for me in mindfulness – or conscientiousness – of expression. I might write something that I think is true, but having written it, and knowing that other people are (hopefully!) going to read it, I then look at it again to make sure. Invariably I have found that, although sort of true, or true in some situations, what I've written does not quite say what I mean, and I have needed to think it through more carefully, more thoroughly, to make it truer. Ethical considerations also come into our reflections on experience, especially reflections on our own behaviour, as we'll see in Chapter 2.

Thought is the welling up of unknown life into consciousness. Although I like the metaphor of reflection, it does have its limitations in describing reflective thought. When we reflect, there is a sense in which we are trying to be like a mirror, reflecting perfectly whatever is in front of us. However, something else can happen too. Mirrors don't reflect deeply, but we can. When we think about something seriously over a period of time, when we concentrate on it, become absorbed in it, aspects of ourselves that we were previously unaware of are pulled into the orbit of our thought, brought into consciousness. Ideas, images, memories, feelings, arise from a deeper level of our being and inform our reflections. We may, for instance, be reflecting on something when we become aware of a subtle feeling of sadness, and we may not at first know why we're feeling this. Did the subject of the reflection cause the sadness, or is there some other cause? We may then reflect on the sadness. Why am I feeling it now? What does it mean? What is it telling me? As we reflect, we may begin to understand that the sadness is, in fact, connected to what we've been reflecting on. Perhaps it reminded us of some personal weakness, or some loss that we have suffered. Before the sadness arose, our reflection was perhaps a little dry and academic, but now we are more fully involved with the reflection. We are more fully present to it.

Or, as we're reflecting on something we may have an idea – a new way of seeing or of doing something occurs to us. We weren't particularly looking for this new idea, it just seemed to pop into our mind, unbidden. When we reflect, we don't just reflect what's in front of us; we recreate our world. We will look at this dimension of reflection in Chapter 3, 'Dwelling on a topic'.

This brings us to the last line of Lawrence's poem: Thought is a man in his wholeness wholly attending. Let's deal first of all with his use of the masculine noun and pronoun – a man in his wholeness – just in case you feel unhappy with the apparent exclusion of women. Lawrence wrote at a time when it was the convention to say man when you meant humanity, although you wouldn't usually have said a man in that case. I would guess though that he meant a human being in their wholeness, or if you prefer, a woman in her wholeness wholly attending.

The ability to attend is essential for reflective thought; in fact, we could say that reflection is simply the ability to attend to the world we live in. So we need to train ourselves to give our full, undivided attention to something, and I'll be suggesting ways we can develop this ability. But Lawrence doesn't just say 'thought is a man wholly attending', he says 'a man in his wholeness wholly attending.' Why the emphasis? I think he is alluding here to depth of attention as well as intensity. It's possible to give something your undivided attention for a while, but with only a certain part of yourself. Other aspects of your being are meanwhile asleep, as it were. For instance, your attention might be fully taken up with a difficult and important task. It really needs to be done right now, and to do it you have to give it your full attention. You can't afford to allow yourself to be distracted by other things. However, completing the task doesn't require your deeper feelings to be involved. In fact, involving them would distract you from the task in hand. So you are wholly attending, but only with a certain part of yourself. You are not a man or woman in your wholeness wholly attending.

The state of wholeness is probably quite rare. It's not often that we need to involve the whole of ourselves in anything. Most of the time we give a part of ourselves to one thing – our job, say – and another part to another thing – our sexual relationship – and another part to something else – our social life – and on the whole this works just fine. We can reflect with just a part of ourselves too, as long as we have enough attention to stay with the topic. Reflecting with the whole of our being has a different quality, though: deeper, stiller, quieter, more penetrating, more loving, more compassionate, more imaginative. We'll be exploring this kind of reflection – what I call contemplation – in the final two chapters of this book, chapters 5 and 6.

Chapter One

······································

A Reflective Life

If you'd seen me leaning on the wall and looking down at the water, you'd have gone, Oh, she's thinking, but I wasn't. I mean, there were words in my head, but just because there are words in your head it doesn't mean you're thinking, just like if you've got a pocket full of pennies it doesn't mean you're rich.[1]

Jess, from the novel *A Long Way Down*,
by Nick Hornby.

I lived for a few years in a Buddhist retreat centre in North Wales, not far from Snowdonia. Sometimes when a friend visited me, if the weather was fine I'd take them to Lake Vyrny, which was about an hour away by car. It's quite a large lake, surrounded by hills, and it has a tree-lined shore. Sometimes the air was very still, and the surface of the lake was also very still, like a mirror reflecting the trees, the hills, and the sky almost perfectly. On days like this I liked to indulge in something a little childish: I liked to bend over so that I could look at the lake upside down. This had an interesting effect. I experienced the illusion that the reflection was the real image, while the real image was the reflection. On other days, however, when there was a breeze, the surface was choppy, so the reflections of the other shore and the sky were all broken up. There were flashes of light and moving fragments of reflection, but no clear picture.

Similarly, the quality of our reflection depends on our state of mind. If it's like the surface of a lake on a windy day then our reflections will be chopped up, broken, fragmentary, with no continuity, and we won't be capable of reflecting what's actually in front of us. We have to learn how to still our minds so that we can think coherently. In a sense we reflect almost all the time, but most of our reflections are disjointed, fragmentary, and undirected. We think about one thing for a little while (maybe a few seconds) and then, in a vague, associative sort of way, we move on to something else, then something else. For instance, you may be reading this but then become aware of a slight pang of hunger and so you start thinking about lunch. Thinking about lunch you remember that you've made an arrangement to meet with a friend for lunch tomorrow. This reminds you that there is something you want to ask your friend about when you see them: you want to ask if there is any truth in the rumour that Richard has split up with his wife and is having an affair with Alice. And this reminds you of a film you saw last week in which Brad Pitt was starring. Now who was the actress?

Two qualities of thinking and two kinds of thought

The language in which the earliest of the Buddha's teachings has come down to us – Pali – has two words to indicate coherent thought: *vitakka* and *vicāra*. *Vitakka* means 'initial thought', and refers to the first moment of attention when your mind initially alights on a subject, while *vicāra* means 'sustained thought', and signifies the continued application of the mind to that subject. These two terms often crop up in the context of meditation, because *vitakka* and *vicāra* are two of the qualities or mental factors present in the state of meditative absorption called in Sanskrit *dhyāna*. (The equivalent term in Pali is *jhāna*, but this is less widely used.) I will say more about *dhyāna* and the factors of meditation later, but for now I will just say a little about initial thought and sustained thought. In the meditation called the mindfulness of breathing, for example, we take our awareness to our breath (this is analogous to initial thought), then we try to keep our awareness on our breath (sustained thought). If you've practised the mindfulness of breathing you'll know that taking your attention to the breath is quite easy, but keeping it there is much more difficult; the mind keeps wandering away from the breath onto other subjects. The initial aim of the meditation is to keep bringing the mind back to the breathing, and in doing so strengthen our capacity for initial and sustained thought.

We can use the *vitakka-vicāra* we've developed in meditation to reflect, by turning our attention from, say, the breath to an idea. This doesn't mean though that we should *only* reflect when we're in *dhyāna* – if that were the case most of us would only be able to reflect very occasionally! But it does suggest a principle: reflection requires a certain amount of calm, peace, and stillness.

Once we've begun to calm our minds a little, what should we reflect on? The answer is simple: anything and everything. We can reflect on the Dharma, of course – on the teachings of the Buddha and other great teachers – but we can also reflect on things that happen to us, on how we respond or react to things that happen to us, on our feelings, on our relationships with other people, on how they respond to what happens to them, on what we read or hear. There's no set syllabus for reflection.

Having said that, we do need to be careful about the kinds of things we think about. Some topics almost invariably catapult us into unskilful states of mind. If you are susceptible to the charms of a certain attractive young person, for instance, thinking about them will probably result in craving, longing, sexual desire. Or if you're prone to depression, dwelling on your shortcomings is likely to send you into a low mood. The Buddha once said, 'Whatever you frequently think and ponder upon, that will become the inclination of your mind.'[2] Expanding on this, he said that before he was Enlightened, he decided to divide his thoughts into two classes. On one side he set thoughts of sensual desire, ill-will, and cruelty (unskilful thoughts) and on the other he set thoughts of renunciation, friendliness, and compassion (skilful thoughts). He discovered that if he allowed himself to dwell in unskilful thoughts they led to suffering, both for him and others. These unskilful thoughts obstructed Wisdom, caused difficulties, and led away from Enlightenment. Consequently, whenever an unskilful thought arose in his mind, he abandoned it. He went on to say that if we allow our minds to dwell on things that cause unskilful states of mind to arise, such as sensual desire, hatred, and cruelty, then that will become the *inclination* of our minds. Conversely, if we allow our minds to dwell on things that cause skilful states of mind to arise, such as renunciation, love, and compassion, then *that* will become the inclination of our minds.

Thoughts can become habitual; we become what we think about. If you allow yourself to have occasional hostile thoughts, if you're not careful, you will become a hostile person. Conversely, if you allow yourself to have friendly thoughts, if you *are* careful, you will become a friendly person. As the Buddha says in the *Dhammapada*:

> Do not underestimate evil, (thinking) 'It will not approach me'. A water-pot becomes full by the (constant) falling drops of water. (Similarly) the spiritually immature person little by little fills himself with evil.

> Do not underestimate good, (thinking) 'It will not approach me'. A water-pot becomes full by the (constant) falling drops of water. (Similarly) the spiritually mature person little by little fills himself with good.[3]

Thinking and not thinking

Coming back to the discourse on the two kinds of thought, the Buddha said that he saw nothing to fear in having skilful thoughts. They didn't lead to his or other's suffering, even if he dwelt in them all day and night. However, he did conclude that it was possible to think and ponder even on skilful things excessively. He found that too much thinking made him tired, and when he was tired he couldn't concentrate. When that happened, he stopped thinking, quietened and steadied his mind, and developed one-pointedness (*ekāgata*). In other words, he meditated.

So in this teaching the Buddha spoke not only about two kinds of thought – skilful and unskilful – but also about two kinds of mental activity: thinking and meditating, or thinking and not-thinking. These two are different, but complementary. Sometimes we need to think about things while at other times we need to stop thinking and still our minds. If we don't still our minds sometimes, through meditation for instance, it will be very hard to reflect: our minds will tend to be like the surface of a lake whipped up into waves by the wind.

On the other hand, if we don't give ourselves time to reflect discursively, we won't be able to meditate effectively. It seems that we *need* to reflect discursively. We need to think about our lives, to process all the impressions we receive, all the things we hear and read, and all our responses to those things. If we don't give ourselves time to do this, we'll probably find that we start thinking about them when we try to meditate. This is perhaps one of the main reasons why some people find meditation difficult – because they don't give themselves time to think. They do all their thinking during meditation time, when they're trying *not* to think! Of course we all have a tendency to distraction, and even if we do give ourselves time to think we may still have some trouble controlling our wayward minds in meditation. However, I'm sure we'd find it easier to meditate if we also gave ourselves time to think.

We also need to learn how to *not* think. Paradoxically, learning how to *not* think is very helpful in developing our ability to think. It's really about having choice: to think effectively and creatively we need to be able to choose not to think; otherwise, our thinking will be compulsive and we'll be at the mercy of whatever thoughts happen to enter our minds. If we're able to not think for a while, that opens up a space in which we can choose what we think about, and when we do think about it, our minds will be clearer, less cluttered with other things vying for our attention. Of course it's very difficult to not think about anything for more than a few seconds simply by force of will. Have a go now and see how long you can do it for! This is where the practice of meditation is very useful. I mentioned above the five factors of the first *dhyāna*. In the second *dhyāna* there are only three factors: rapture, bliss and one-pointedness. *Vitakka* and *vicāra* disappear – that is, there is no longer any thought. This isn't a state of unconsciousness; in fact you feel more aware and alive than ever. It's a state in which you experience the flow of life without 'talking to yourself' about it, that is, without interpreting your experience in words. With practice we can learn to quieten our minds at any time, perhaps not to the point of having no thoughts at all, but at least being able to slow them down, having less frequent thoughts, with longer gaps of silence in between them.

Words and experience

This experience is important because we think with concepts, and concepts are usually expressed in words.[4] An important aspect of thinking is to understand that the words we use are not the things themselves. The word 'cup' is not itself a cup, it's just a sound or a few lines on a piece of paper that, by common consent among English-speaking people, refers to an object that we drink from. This, of course, is obvious, but it is easy to forget, and when we do forget it then we're no longer thinking about real things or experiences, we're thinking about concepts and words. It's quite interesting to look at the printed word 'cup' for a while and see what happens. When I look at it I begin to realize how automatically, unconsciously and quickly (instantaneously it seems) my mind transforms those three shapes – c u p – made of black lines on a white background, into a symbol for something else, something I can hold in my hands and drink from. Now that I stop and look at the three letters for a while a funny thing happens. The thing that those shapes symbolize (a thing that I drink from) sort of drops away, and now I experience a strange ambiguity. On the one hand they are just shapes, but at the same time they symbolize the thing that I drink from. Before I stopped to really look at the shapes I had automatically and unconsciously turned those shapes into a concept, an idea, a symbol, of something else (a thing that I drink from). I had forgotten, or overlooked, the fact that all I was looking at were the three shapes of black on white. It was as if the three shapes c u and p *were* in fact the thing that I drink from.

A similar thing happens when you *say* a word over and over again. Have a go at saying 'cup' over and over again and see what happens to it. If you're like me, at first you think of a thing you drink from; perhaps you see one in your imagination. After a while though, the thing that you drink from falls away and you're just left with the sound of the back of your mouth making the c, your throat making the u, and your lips making the p. You can also *feel* the back of your mouth making the c sound, and so on. Weird, isn't it? What's happening is that we're uncoupling the shapes on the page, or the sounds we make, from the thing, or experience, that those shapes or sounds usually symbolize. That is, we're seeing that the shapes or the sounds can symbolize something else, but they are not the thing they symbolize.

The philosopher Arthur Schopenhauer emphasized the importance of referring our words to actual lived experience. He thought that a lot of what was called philosophy in his day was merely playing with concepts rather than thinking about real life. He wrote: 'Concepts always remain universal, and so do not reach down to the particular; yet it is precisely the particular that has to be dealt with in life.'[5] He went on to say that concepts stand in the same sort of relation to living experience as a copy in mosaic does to a painting in oils:

> However fine the mosaic may be, the edges of the
> stones always remain, so that no continuous transition
> from one tint to another is possible. In the same way,
> concepts, with their rigidity and sharp delineation,
> however finely they may be split by closer definition, are
> always incapable of reaching the fine modifications of
> perception.[6]

The Buddha also spoke about the mind's tendency to get caught in conceptualization divorced from direct experience. He said that, based on the contact between our physical senses (sight, sound, touch etc.) and our environment, we experience feelings about that contact – pleasant, unpleasant or neutral (somewhere in between pleasant and unpleasant). Our perception of the world consists of these two elements: contact with our environment and feelings about it. We then think about our perceptions – 'That feels good, I like that, how can I prolong this experience or get more of it?', or 'That was unpleasant, I didn't like it, how can I stop having this experience and make sure I don't have any more of it in the future?' In other words, our thinking is based on craving for the pleasant and aversion to the unpleasant. It also involves ideas of past and future, because in order to avoid experiences that we didn't like or repeat experiences that we did, we have to remember how they happened, and then plan for the future. Once we start thinking in this way our mind proliferates ideas, fantasies, plans, strategies and so on, and this distracts us from our direct perception. Rather than simply perceiving things as they are – some pleasant, some unpleasant, some neutral – we think about how we can maximize our pleasure and minimize our pain. The Buddha called this proliferation of ideas *papañca*. To summarize: there is *contact* between the senses and our environment ⟶ *feelings* (pleasant, unpleasant or neutral) ⟶ *perception* ⟶ *thoughts* ⟶ *mental proliferation (papañca)*.[7]

In the diagram overleaf ,[8] the left-hand triangle represents our direct perception of the world as experienced through our senses. The right-hand (upside-down) triangle represents our thinking mind. The more we experience the world directly through our senses, the less we experience it through the medium of concepts, because when we pay attention to our senses there is simply less room left in our mind for thoughts. This is illustrated in the diagram. The lower end of the diagram shows a thicker band of sensory awareness and a thinner band of conceptualization, with no thinking at all at the bottom – just direct perception. The higher part of the diagram shows a very 'thin', tenuous perception of the environment, and a lot of conceptualization – our brains work overtime when we're not in touch with our senses! This is the high point of *papañca*!

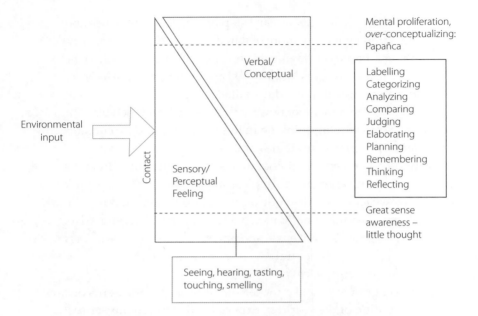

Environmental input → Contact

Verbal/Conceptual

Sensory/Perceptual Feeling

Mental proliferation, *over*-conceptualizing: Papañca

Labelling
Categorizing
Analyzing
Comparing
Judging
Elaborating
Planning
Remembering
Thinking
Reflecting

Great sense awareness – little thought

Seeing, hearing, tasting, touching, smelling

When we operate from the upper end of the diagram – that is, when our thinking is mainly conceptual, with little or no grounding in direct experience – we're not thinking about real things and experiences, we're thinking about words and concepts. Let's look once again at those three little shapes c u and p. Now think of a cup. Actually, what would be really good at this point would be if you could go and get a cup so that you can hold it in your hands and look at it. I know that if there isn't a cup nearby it will be a bother to go and get one, but it would really help me to make the point if you did that. So now, looking at the cup, notice its shape and colour or colours, and the way the light falls on one part of it, while another part is slightly shaded. If it has a shiny finish, notice the reflections on different parts of its surface. Now turn your attention to the feeling of the cup in your hands: the texture, the temperature, the shape. If it's empty, look inside. Can you begin to see how that simple word 'cup' doesn't even begin to do justice to the experience of actually holding one in your hand and looking at it? The word 'cup' is a very simplified shorthand for an experience that is multi-faceted, multi-dimensional and – quite wonderful.

And I wonder what sort of cup you have been holding, either in your mind or literally? Was it white, made of china, quite small, and a sort of half-circle shape? Or maybe it was brown, made of clay, quite large, and shaped like a funnel? Or was it orange plastic and tube-shaped? Probably none of those. Yet they're all called 'cup'. So the word 'cup' symbolizes a number of quite different objects; like all words, 'cup' is very general and unspecific. Even when we give it more characteristics, as when we say white, china, small, in the shape of a half-circle – the cup I'm imagining is probably still quite different from the one you're holding or imagining. Perhaps this doesn't matter very much when it comes to cups, but consider the consequences if we make this mistake about some other things, such as men, women, homosexuals, heterosexuals, black, white, Americans, Arabs, Muslims (Sunnis, Shias), Jews, Hindus, Christians (Catholics, Protestants), terrorists, freedom-fighters, bombs, democracy, torture, war. It becomes a bit frightening, doesn't it? The Buddha said that *papañca* leads to conflict, disputes, argumentation, and violence, and it's not difficult to see why. Based on our experience of some things being pleasant and others unpleasant, we develop craving and aversion. The experiences that we like or dislike are then conceptualized, and therefore generalized: an experience we've had stands for a general class of things. As soon as we do that we are on very shaky ground, because, to repeat Schopenhauer: 'Concepts always remain universal, and so do not reach down to the particular; yet it is precisely the particular that has to be dealt with in life.' It is easy to be misled by our categories, assuming that they are really existing things, and then to act on that mistake.

So we need to be careful when we reflect that we're not merely *papañcizing*! We need to try to keep our thinking as close as we can to what we know through direct experience. Of course we have to use concepts, but it's important to hold them lightly and provisionally, remembering that while they can be useful, they cannot adequately describe the way things are. We must also try to make sure that our reflections are *disinterested*, remembering that this doesn't mean *uninterested*, but *unbiased* by personal interest or advantage.

Meditation, reflection, and action

Let's return to the Buddha's discourse on the two kinds of thought – skilful and unskilful – and about the two kinds of mental activity – meditating and reflecting. He was talking to *bhikkhus* when he spoke about these: disciples who had left home and who spent most of their time meditating and reflecting. Most people reading this book will be in a very different situation: earning a living, looking after a family, shopping, cleaning, paying bills, etc. So we don't have just two things to balance, we have three: meditation, reflection, and action. Balancing these three is very difficult because earning a living, looking after a family etc., are very time-consuming. In Alexander McCall Smith's novel *Friends, Lovers, Chocolate*, Isabel Dalhousie – moral philosopher, editor of the *Journal of Applied Philosophy* and occasional detective – looks after her niece's delicatessen for a week, while she (Cat) is on holiday. After Isabel spends a morning cutting cheese, wrapping bread and serving customers, McCall Smith writes:

> So the morning drifted by, and not once, she reflected,
> had she had the opportunity to think about moral
> philosophy. This was cause for thought: most people
> led their lives this way – doing rather than thinking;
> they acted, rather than thought about acting. This made
> philosophy a luxury – the privilege of those who did not
> have to spend their time cutting cheese and wrapping
> bread. From the perspective of the cheese counter,
> Schopenhauer seemed far away.[9]

A few years ago it was commonly thought that with all the ingenious labour-saving devices that scientists were inventing, we were entering an age of leisure. This hasn't happened. In fact, people in the West work more hours now than they did when those predictions were made.[10] Some of the ingenious devices that have been invented, such as email, the mobile phone and the Blackberry, have actually increased many people's working hours. Checking work emails at home and conducting business meetings on the phone when on the train or walking down the street are

The Art of Reflection

common.[11] Work isn't the only culprit though – personal use of the internet and the mobile phone take up a lot of our leisure time too. Have you noticed how activity of any kind has a tendency to take up more and more time, like a fast-growing weed taking over the whole of the garden? In the eleventh century in Tibet Atiśa said: 'There is never an end of things to do, so limit your activities,'[12] and that was before the phone, TV, internet and Blackberry were invented! It's even more important today to resist the tendency of activity to colonize our time.

I'm not saying that activity is bad or unspiritual, just that most people I know find it hard to make time for meditation and reflection. A few years ago I came across a very useful distinction between the urgent and the important. The urgent consists of things that have to be done right now, or at least very soon. The important is made up of things that you value – friendship, loved ones, meaningful activities, reading, listening to music, self-development, etc. The urgent has a tendency to take precedence over the important; that is, we tend to keep putting off the important things in our lives because there are always urgent matters to be seen to. We have to make a real effort to make sure we have time for the important things in our lives, otherwise one day we'll die without ever having got round to them!

Of course it's possible to reflect in the midst of activity, and we often do. In fact, ideally we wouldn't have these hard and fast distinctions; we'd meditate as we work and reflect as we clean our house. The Buddha once spoke about the importance of maintaining a balance between activity and formal practice. He was talking about the qualities of a Stream Entrant (without going into technical details, let's just say that a Stream Entrant is a quite advanced practitioner of the Dharma). He said that one of the characteristics of a Stream Entrant is that no matter how busy they are, no matter how much they may do for others, they never forget their training in ethics, meditation, and wisdom ('wisdom' here meaning the practice of reflection). He used a simile to make his point: a cow with a calf will always keep an eye on her calf as she grazes. In this simile the grazing is the various activities we engage in and the calf is our training in ethics, meditation, and wisdom.[13]

Getting started on reflection

I want to conclude this chapter by suggesting ways you might get started on learning how to reflect. First of all, you have to learn how to do nothing! This is absolutely essential. By doing nothing I don't mean watching the TV, listening to the radio, or reading the newspaper. I don't even mean reading a good book, not even a Buddhist one. I mean literally doing nothing. And turn off your mobile phone and computer. Make time to do nothing every day – perhaps start with ten minutes a day, then, once you get used to that, extend it to twenty, thirty minutes, even an hour! *Make* time or it probably won't happen. Put it in your diary. Sometimes, when I'm trying to arrange a meeting with someone, or if I'm asked to do something at a certain time, I'll look at my diary and see that I'm doing nothing at that time, so I'll say 'Sorry, I'm unavailable then.' They might then ask me what I'm doing, and I'll say 'Nothing'.

> Incomprehension: 'So you *can* meet me then?'
> 'No.'
> 'But you said you weren't doing anything then.'
> 'No, I said I was doing nothing.'

My friends have got used to this, but I have to explain to people who don't know me very well that doing nothing is an important activity that I'm not willing to give up easily.

We can't reflect in a hurry. We need to feel that we have 'all the time in the world', because deeper understanding happens in its own time. If we want to learn how to reflect, we first need to learn how to do nothing, because it's out of the spaciousness of doing nothing that our minds can open out. This spaciousness allows our mind to range freely and unhurriedly around and through whatever it is that we've chosen to consider. We need to have a sense of timelessness. I don't mean that we enter into the infinite (although we may do!), but that we *feel* that we have all the time in the world, that there is nothing for us to do, that it's OK to do nothing, to achieve nothing. You might think that you don't have the time for this, and if that's the case it might be a good thing to take a look at your life to see if there is anything you can cut out, because having time to do nothing is important. However, entering into the 'timeless realm' doesn't necessarily require a lot of time. 'Timeless' doesn't mean 'lots of time'. We need to *feel* that we have all the time in the world, even though we may not – because, of course, we never do. We enter the timeless realm when we give up looking for results, when we stop trying to meet targets and deadlines, when we cease to think of time as a commodity. If we've only got ten minutes to spare we can enter into the timeless realm, as long as we don't try to fill that time up with something useful. Reflection is not useful. To reflect we need to feel free – we need to feel that it's OK to be totally useless.

In an essay called *Sitting Still*, Walter Murdoch wrote:

> Let us make up our minds that in the coming year we will sit about . . . more than we have done in the past. This is not, as you might hastily conclude, a plea for laziness. Thinking is the hardest work in the world; most of us are too lazy to attempt it. We prefer what we call the Strenuous Life, which means being busy and fussy, and joining a dozen committees, and imagining that we are doing a great deal of good in the world, and blinding ourselves to the fact that we are all suffering from St Vitus's Dance – a disease which we can cure only by shaking off our laziness and acquiring the difficult art of sitting still.[14]

Many people find it very difficult to do nothing. They get jumpy, they fall asleep, they feel guilty, or have an uneasy feeling that they should be doing something. If you feel this way I suggest making a cup of tea. OK, making a cup of tea is not doing nothing exactly, but tea, I find, is very conducive to reflection. Look at the cup, at the liquid, the steam rising from the cup, the reflections on the surface of the tea. Feel the heat of the cup on your hands, taste the tea. We're so accustomed to the idea that we should always be doing something useful that we often continue with our activity while we're drinking our tea. Or we use the ten minutes of our tea break to do something else, something useful. What a terrible habit! Try being useless instead – at least for a few minutes. Look at something: a vase of flowers, a plant, the view out of your window, your feet. Listen to sounds.

As you sit doing nothing, thoughts will occur to you. Notice what things you think about – you can learn a lot about yourself that way. Do you think about cars, food, sex, football, *The X-Factor*, films, music, literature, philosophy, other people, yourself, the Dharma, or what? Remember what the Buddha said: 'Whatever you frequently think and ponder upon, that will become the inclination of your mind.' When a thought occurs to you, try to choose whether or not to follow it. Most of the time we're at the mercy of whatever subject happens to present itself to us: we're not so much thinking as being thought. We have to learn to make choices.

In the case of some topics, it's not that we necessarily need to stop thinking about them. It may be that we need to think about them in a different way. Try to reflect on things from a Dharmic perspective. What do I mean by that? We have *our* perception of things, and there is the way an Enlightened person would perceive them. When we reflect from a Dharmic perspective, we try to see things *as if* we were Enlightened. For example, you may have noticed that you're looking older. Perhaps you have a few grey hairs that weren't there before or the 'crow's feet' around your eyes are a little more pronounced. Perhaps you're a little more prone to fat around the stomach and you're not quite as good-looking as you used to be. There are a number of trains of thought that could come from this. You could, for instance, worry about it or get depressed. You could start thinking about what you could do to slow down the ageing process: perhaps enrol in a gym or go to your local health shop and buy some vitamins and creams. You could start thinking about ways to disguise the effect of ageing on your appearance: cosmetics, hair dye, clothes with a different cut to disguise your growing stomach. You might even consider cosmetic surgery.

Alternatively, you could think about the ageing process – *your* ageing process – from a Dharmic perspective. You might use it as an opportunity to develop insight. 'I'm growing old. I'm moving towards death. All conditioned things are impermanent, including me. What does this mean? What is the significance of life? Why are we born only to grow old and die? What is the point of it all?' In this way, instead of the fact of our ageing being something unpleasant, unwelcome, to be dismissed from the mind or fought against, it can be an opportunity for liberation.

Regular Dharma study helps us to look at things from this Dharmic perspective. Whenever we think about things, we think about them from a certain point of view, and we're not usually aware of our point of view. We've learned to look at things in a particular way from our parents, our teachers at school, our friends, the society we grew up in, the entertainment industry. Often, we don't realize that it's the *way* we look at things – the point of view from which we look – that's the problem. Ageing, for instance, is only a problem if you want to remain young forever. (That *is* a problem because you can't remain young forever.) Ageing itself isn't a problem but your desire to remain young is. You can't stop the ageing process. You may be able to slow it down a little, or at least cover over its effects for a while, but eventually you will get old, unless of course you die before that! But you *can* change your attitude; you can transform your desire to remain young into a desire for wisdom.

Three things to remember when reflecting

First: when you first start your practice of doing nothing, you may not enjoy it very much. You may in fact find it unpleasant, and you may wonder why you're doing it. As in some other activities, you have to work at it. Effort comes first, enjoyment later. If you're used to listening to rock music for instance, listening to classical music is not very easy; it sounds alien, and is not very enjoyable: 'Where are the drums and bass?' However, if you persist, the beauty of classical music begins to reveal itself and you start to enjoy it.

Second: reflecting is not worrying! Many people are anxious by nature and when they have nothing else to do they start worrying about things – all sorts of things. I know because I'm one of them! So, if you're like me you have to beware of this and not to fall into worrying. Be careful not to obsess on a topic – going round and round, not getting anywhere, just getting into a more and more anxious state. I've found that if I make sure that I have time to do nothing, I am less prone to anxiety.[15]

Third: time spent on reflection is never wasted; it always bears fruit. You may think that I'm now contradicting something I wrote above, where I said that time spent doing nothing is a useless activity. Now I'm saying that it is never time wasted. But the contradiction is only apparent. It depends on what you mean by useful or useless. Time spent reflecting won't get the mortgage paid, won't get the shopping done, won't get the house clean. It won't show any tangible results. But it *will* help you to get to know yourself. It will help you to deepen your experience of yourself, make you calmer and more positive, clarify your mind and help you understand life better. Reflection will make you wiser.

Chapter Two

....

Learning from Experience

What is the good of experience if you do not reflect?[1]

Frederick the Great

My earliest memory is of something that happened on my fifth birthday. My parents had arranged a party, and we invited a few of my friends to the bungalow we lived in. I don't remember very much about it; no doubt there was cake and jelly and lemonade and party games and laughter, but I don't remember any of that. What I remember is going into the bathroom to have a pee. I could hear the excited shouting and laughter outside, in the living room, but it was relatively quiet in the bathroom once I'd closed the door. The sudden contrast, from being absorbed in the fun and games of the party to being alone in the quiet, shocked me into self-awareness, and I remember thinking 'I am me'. I may even have said it out loud. I realized my separateness, and I felt a sort of serene but mysterious excitement. Mysterious because there was something strange and slightly scary in being alive, alone, and separate.

Plato famously said that philosophy begins with a sense of wonder; and the sense of wonder arises from self-awareness. But reflection isn't a special activity undertaken only by intellectuals and philosophers. Everyone reflects, at least sometimes, because self-awareness is inherently reflective – it's awareness bending or turning back on itself. Young children are always asking questions, aren't they? Some of them are relatively easy to answer: What is a train? Why does Daddy shave? Where do birds live? Why do I

have to go to school? (Hmm, maybe not always so easy to answer!)
Other questions are more difficult: Where did I come from? Where
would I be if I hadn't been born? Why am I me, and not you?
These kinds of questions arise out of the child's experience of
self-awareness. We seem to 'grow out of' these questions as we
get older, and perhaps we now consider them to be naïve and
childish, but it *is* weird being alive, isn't it? Why *am* I me and
not you?

Meditative thought

I mentioned in Chapter 1 the Buddha's 'two kinds of thought':
skilful and unskilful. The philosopher Martin Heidegger
also spoke about two kinds of thought, although these are
different from the Buddha's: Heidegger's are calculative and
meditative thinking.[2] Calculative thinking plans, organizes,
solves problems, looks for results. Meditative thinking is more
open. When we think meditatively we don't have an end result
in mind; we're not trying to work something out or find a
solution to a problem. We're just thinking because we want
to, because we're curious, and because it's enjoyable to watch
something reveal itself to us. Pay attention to anything and it
becomes interesting: a beetle, a cloud, a stone, a breath, an idea.
What are they? How do they work? How are they related to
the things around them?

In Chapter 1 we briefly met Isabel Dalhousie, Alexander
McCall Smith's fictional philosopher. There are a number
of books in the *Isabel Dalhousie* series, and they offer some
wonderful examples of meditative thinking – they're really
vehicles for McCall Smith's humane and wise reflections on life.
Isabel reflects throughout the novels about everyday things:
current events, fashions, things that people do and say, and her
own actions. Sometimes her reflections are about serious moral
or personal issues, while at other times they are playful. Here's
a playful passage that turns into a reflection on mortality, while
remaining playful:

Her desk was piled with manuscripts, the consequence of her dogged adherence to a policy of requiring the submission of articles in printed, rather than electronic, form. She could not read on screen, or at least not for long; the sentences and paragraphs became strangely disjointed, as if they were cut off from that which went before and that which came afterwards. That, of course, was an illusion; such paragraphs were just round the corner, just a scroll away – but where was that? Was electronic memory a *place?* Before they appeared on the screen weren't they just endless lines of noughts and ones, or odd decimals? That, she thought, was the ultimate triumph of reductionism: Shakespeare's sonnets could be reduced to rows of noughts; or even the work of Proust; although how much electricity would be consumed to render Proust's long-winded prose digital? Patient wind turbines would turn and turn for days in that process. And what about ourselves, and our own reduction? We could each be rendered, could we not, down to a little puddle of water and a tiny heap of minerals. *Imperial Caesar, dead, and turned to clay, Might stop a hole to keep the wind away.* Or, as binary code might prosaically put it: 010010010110110110 1110000 . . .[3]

Not that reflection consists only in meditative thinking – there's a place for calculative thinking too. Self-awareness comes with its own problems. If we weren't self-aware we'd just get on with life, doing what we do without thinking about it, as animals seem to do. Self-awareness allows us to stand back, as it were, from what we're doing so that we can evaluate our behaviour: we notice that we're thinking or behaving in a certain way, and perhaps see that it's not the best way to think or behave. We can imagine thinking or behaving differently, but we often find it very difficult to do. Self-awareness is inherently problematic. 'The problem with being me, thought Isabel . . . is that I keep thinking about the problem of being me.'[4] Problems such as: Why did I have that huge row with my girlfriend over something so trivial?

Why do I do things that I know are bad for me? Why didn't I do what I promised to do? Why do I dislike my colleague so intensely? Why do I feel lonely sometimes? Questions like these probably occur to us all, but we don't always reflect on them for very long; perhaps because we're not interested enough, or because they are unpleasant, or because we feel we haven't got time, or because it's hard work, or because we don't think we'll be able to come up with an answer. Reflection is simply the giving of time to the questions that occur to you.

This is partly a matter of temperament. Some people like being alone and enjoy thinking about things, while others prefer company and activity. I'm the kind of person who enjoys solitude and reflection – that's why I've come to be writing this book – but I'm aware that this doesn't suit everyone. I didn't write this book because I wanted everyone to be like me, but to encourage people to reflect a little more on the questions, problems, setbacks, and hurts that we all encounter in our daily lives. By doing that we learn about ourselves, about other people, and about the world.

Reflection is always personal

Another philosopher, Gabriel Marcel, once described how the roots of reflection lie in the very ordinary experience of having a problem.[5] He gave a very simple example to show what he meant. Imagine that you've mislaid your watch. As soon as you become aware that it's missing it, what do you do? You try to remember when and where you last had it. You recollect the last few hours – what were you doing, where were you? Was it this morning at breakfast? Yes, perhaps it was. So you go back to the table and there it is – reflection has helped you solve the problem.

Marcel says that two important factors caused you to reflect in this way. First, you experienced a 'slight shock' on first noticing that the watch was missing, which made you stop what you were doing. 'Reflection,' he says, 'is attention directed towards a small break in the daily chain of habit'. Second, the watch is valuable, you want to find it, so it's worth thinking about. 'Reflection is never exercised on things that are not worth the trouble of reflecting about.' There's no point in trying to reflect on something that doesn't interest you; your mind will just wander off onto something more interesting. It has to matter to you.

This means that reflection is always *personal*. It was *your* watch, and *you* left it on the table; no-one else could have reflected for you. In a similar way, the questions you reflect on are questions for *you*, so *you* have to answer them. Of course, sometimes a question has a simple answer, and someone may answer it for you – someone may have seen your watch and can tell you where it is. But some questions don't have easy answers, or the answers you're given don't satisfy you, or they lead to further questions.

Marcel goes on to show how a similar process to the scenario with the watch can apply to your inner life. Imagine that you're talking to a friend and you somehow let yourself be drawn into telling a lie. Later, recalling this incident, you feel upset because you consider yourself to be an honest person. Once again, there is the slight shock – 'a break in the daily chain of habit' – that makes you reflect. 'How was it possible for me to tell such a whopper?' And once again, something valuable to you is at stake. You see yourself as an honest person, so you can't go on as if nothing had happened. In reflecting on this lie you're forced to reflect on yourself. Perhaps you're not really the person you thought you were?

Marcel's third example goes a step further. A friend has done something which has disappointed you. However, as you think about this, you remember a time when you did something similar, and this makes you ask: 'Was this act of mine really so very different from the act which today I feel inclined to judge so severely? But in that case am I in any position to condemn my friend?' Your reflection now calls *you* into question – are you really in a position to judge your friend harshly?

Such a reflection will of course be painful, but Marcel makes a very interesting point about this. As well as the anguish you will no doubt be feeling, you may also 'have a certain sense of being set free', as if you'd overturned some obstruction in your way. There are two aspects to that freedom. Firstly, you're able to communicate at a broader level with yourself now that you have 'introduced the self that committed the dubious act to the self that did not hesitate to set itself up as the harsh judge of such acts in others'. Secondly, you are able to enter into more intimate communication with your friend, since between you 'there no longer stands that barrier which separates the judge on the bench from the accused man in the dock.'

The difficulty of seeing ourselves as we are

Marcel's examples of reflection are models of self-honesty. It's natural to try to avoid such home truths because to admit to them is unpleasant. There's a syndrome recognized in psychology called 'perceptual defence', which is a strategy we use for avoiding certain truths or ideas that threaten us in some way: we simply don't perceive them. In an experiment carried out in 1946 some people watched a screen on which words were projected for a very short time – so short that they weren't registered consciously. The words continued to be flashed for increasingly longer periods until the subjects were able to 'see' them consciously. The interesting thing is that some of the words were neutral, others vulgar or disturbing, and the subjects were able to see the neutral words much sooner than they saw the vulgar or disturbing ones.[6] In a similar way, we often fail to see the more negative aspects of ourselves, because to do so would be painful. One psychologically astute Tibetan definition of ignorance is: 'a stubborn closed-mindedness about learning anything that you feel might threaten your ego-identity, and upset the sense of security you wish to get from it, but which you are unaware of, and therefore feel you must protect'.[7]

How do we get beyond our perceptual defence, our 'stubborn closed-mindedness', to see ourselves more honestly? In the study I quoted earlier, the subjects did eventually recognize the disturbing and vulgar words that were being projected onto the screen. They couldn't ignore them indefinitely. Similarly, if you frequently reflect on your experience, you begin to notice that your view of yourself doesn't quite add up. You can't help noticing inconsistencies between the way you like to think of yourself and your behaviour. Perhaps you consider yourself to be a kind person, for instance, yet you just spoke quite harshly to someone; or you think that you're quite mature, yet you just did something very childish. Usually we overlook these inconsistencies, but reflection brings them into awareness.

It can be revealing to reflect on the way you think of yourself. Perhaps you see yourself as a cheerful person, someone who always looks on the bright side of life, the life and soul of the party. Or perhaps you're a quiet, thoughtful person, someone for whom still waters run deep. Or perhaps you're a maverick – someone who goes their own way, disregarding the rules and conventions, like one of those detectives in a TV series. Whatever image you have of yourself, it's probably not true, or at least not completely true. In fact, you're probably the opposite as well. People who are constantly cheerful, for instance, often have a darker, sadder, aspect of their personality, which they don't allow into consciousness. That's one of the reasons why some cheerful people can be irritating – because we intuit that they're playing a part rather than being fully themselves. Of course this isn't only the case with the determinedly cheerful; we all have a self-image, a role that we tend to play, which ultimately confines us, because we're much bigger than our conscious identity can hold. 'I am large. I contain multitudes,' as Walt Whitman wrote.[8]

The importance of positive emotions

However, the main obstacle to self-knowledge is emotional. Learning about unacknowledged negative aspects of ourselves is unpleasant. Our self-esteem takes a knock; we feel insecure because we're no longer so certain of who we are and where we stand in the world. There's also a sense of loss – the loss of a cherished idea of ourselves we may have had. So we also need to work on the emotional level, developing positive emotions such as appreciation and gratitude, loving kindness and compassion. Positive emotions give us the inner resources to deal with the emotional upset of seeing aspects of ourselves that we don't like.

There are a number of meditation practices in the Buddhist tradition whose purpose is to help us develop positive emotions. The Development of Loving Kindness (Mettā Bhāvanā) is a good example. There are five stages to the practice. In the first stage we try to cultivate a feeling of loving kindness (metta) towards ourselves; in the second stage towards a friend; in the third stage, someone we don't know very well; and in the fourth stage towards an 'enemy'. In the fifth stage we try to develop an equal degree of goodwill towards all four people, and then we gradually extend this feeling outwards as far as we can, including non-human beings. By repeatedly practising this meditation we gradually become friendlier and kinder, the protective emotional barriers that separate us from others dissolve, and a sense of well-being and warm connection with the whole of life becomes established within us. One of the many benefits of developing metta is that we become less dependent on other people's opinions of us. Our sense of well-being and value begins to be based on love and connectedness rather than status, power, beauty, skill, or competence. The problem with basing our sense of worth on any of the latter is that they depend on comparison. If I am better than, or at least as good as others, I feel OK about myself, but I also run the risk of being in a situation in which I am the worst in the class, in which case I will feel bad.

Most of us are very good at avoiding this unpleasant experience though. There has been quite a lot of research that shows that the majority of people over-estimate their positive qualities, think that they are above average in most areas of life, and tend to interpret events in ways that maintain an image of themselves as being competent, capable and good![9] I enjoy watching football on the TV, and it can be very amusing to see the team managers' reactions to disputed decisions by the referee. If the ref gives a penalty in a case that is arguable, for instance, then the manager of the side who had the penalty awarded against them will argue vociferously against the decision, with great indignation and a sense of injustice. (They always seem to forget that their team had a penalty awarded in their favour in a similarly arguable case not so long ago.)

Meanwhile the manager of the other team will calmly agree with the ref's decision, or at best say that they weren't close enough to see it. Not once have I seen a manager whose team has been awarded a dubious penalty admit that the penalty shouldn't have been given. Sometimes I get the impression that they know the truth of the matter but are unwilling to admit it. At other times though, they seem to really believe that they are right, even when they are clearly wrong. Their view of reality is strongly biased in their team's favour. Football managers' partisanship is only an extreme case of what we all tend to do – look at the world with a strong bias in our favour. Of course football managers of teams that are regularly on the TV have a lot at stake: they are paid colossal amounts of money and they can easily lose their job if their team doesn't do well. Most of us don't have as much to lose. In fact, what *do* we stand to lose if we admit that we're wrong, or have failed, or have behaved badly? We lose the good feelings we get from being right, successful and well-behaved. We feel bad.

Positive emotions such as loving kindness help us to feel happy in ourselves even when we're proven wrong or have failed at something. Rather than needing to prove ourselves by being capable, successful, right etc., we need instead to learn to love ourselves and others. When we are in a loving state of mind, our and others' relative skills and competencies are of little concern. Positive emotions also reduce our self-preoccupation. Loving kindness and compassion naturally make us more concerned about others, so that our personal concerns seem less important. From this perspective our feeling of upset on seeing a previously unacknowledged weakness is not so important. When we're aware of other people's suffering, does it really matter that we're not quite as good as we thought we were?

Reflection then is as much to do with emotion as it is to do with reason. The more emotionally positive we are, the freer and more penetrating our reflections will be. That's one of the reasons why the experience of *dhyāna* is important: it's an intense and deep experience of positive emotion that allows us to see truths that we've previously avoided because of their threat to our sense of security. So the more *dhyāna* we experience, the further we can go with reflection, because our ability to 'see' is less hampered by the need to protect ourselves from unpleasant truths.

Selflessness

Eventually we might even realize that our concern with ourselves is a mistaken enterprise. Ultimately there is no-one to protect. This is the Buddha's famous *anattā* – no-self – doctrine. He said that our ego-identity, or self-view, is merely an image, an idea, or a set of ideas, about who we are and what we're like. It's a story, a narrative, that we continually tell ourselves, and that gives us a consistent sense of identity: 'My name is Ratnaguna, I'm male, middle-aged, a father, a teacher, intelligent, honest, overly critical, quick tempered . . .' etc. But our sense of ourselves feels more substantial than a few ideas, doesn't it? It feels as if it's something real, something actually existing. And it feels very important that we protect it. It's even a matter of life or death sometimes; people have killed to protect their sense of identity when it's been under threat. According to psychologist Mark Leary, most people have the sense that their self resides just behind and between the eyes:

> If you are like most people, you may have the vague
> sense that there is, inside your head, a small,
> experiencing 'thing' that registers your experience,
> thinks your thoughts and feels your feelings – some sort
> of conscious entity 'in there' that is the centre of your
> awareness, thought and conscious experience. Many
> people report that this mental presence is at the core
> of whom they really or most essentially are, and some
> people have the sense that their body is just a vehicle for
> carrying around this important mental entity. For some
> people, the constant presence of this sense of self is what
> convinces them that they are the same person today
> as they were many years ago. Despite all the changes
> that they have experienced, this inner self has remained
> constant.[10]

I suppose people feel that their self resides just behind the eyes because they look out at the world from their eyes, and so they feel they must exist just behind them! I'm more inclined to feel that my self exists somewhere in my chest, in the region of the heart. Wherever we feel it to be though, there does seem to be a self, a centre of control and awareness, somewhere inside us. Isn't that what I experienced in the bathroom on my fifth birthday? Isn't that what we mean by self-awareness? So when the Buddha tells us that in reality there is no self, doesn't that contradict our experience?

Now we need to be clear about what the Buddha claimed did not exist. We have our experience of living in this world – tasting, touching, hearing, smelling, seeing, pleasure and pain – and he didn't deny this experience. How could he? That would be absurd – of course we exist! But we don't only *have* experience. We also *interpret* our experience, and our interpretations happen so quickly that we don't realize that we're interpreting. We think our interpretations are experiences. (So the idea of reflecting on our experience is more difficult than we might at first realize.) According to the Buddha there is one particular interpretation that causes a lot of trouble and unnecessary suffering: that of a self at the centre of our experience. He said that if we look closely enough we'll see that our actual experience is simply a flow of ever-changing sensations, feelings and thoughts. But because there's continuity in this experience – we feel pretty much like the same person from day to day – we assume there's a self doing the experiencing.

The idea of a self works perfectly well for practical purposes, such as telling someone that they're standing on your toes or buying tickets for the cinema. It would be tiresome to have to say 'Please, that foot is standing on these toes', or 'It would be agreeable to see the 6.40 showing of *Apocalypse Now*'. Wouldn't it? It's so much easier and more sensible to say 'Excuse me, you are standing on my toes' and 'I'd like to buy a ticket, please', even though, in reality, there is no you or me. The idea of a self only causes trouble and suffering to the extent that we assume that there is more to it than a linguistic convention, a way of speaking.

And we do. We assume there is something really there, and then we feel a need to protect it, cherish it, have ambitions for it, and feel assured that it stands up pretty well compared to other selves – above average, actually!

A few paragraphs back I gave a brief outline of a meditation practice called the Development of Loving Kindness, the first stage of which consists in developing loving kindness towards oneself. But if there's no self, how can we feel loving kindness towards it? What we're really doing is developing loving kindness towards this flow of ever-changing sensations, feelings and thoughts, but again, for practical purposes, we use the idea of a self. It's just a way of speaking. It's a kind of abbreviation, and isn't meant to imply that there really is a self. Positive emotions in fact help us to realize that the self is not an experience but an interpretation, because they are less self-ish than negative emotions. When we feel loving kindness, or compassion, or gratitude, or sympathy, we feel softer, less hard-edged, more expansive, as concerned for others as we usually are for ourselves. From there it is a fairly short step to realize that our sense of separateness is illusory, that it doesn't really reflect our experience. This means that when we're in an emotionally positive state we're closer to our actual experience, closer to reality, in a better position to see through the interpretation of a self, than when we're in a negative state. So the next time you feel friendly and loving, all you need to do is reflect on the meaning, the significance of your experience, and you may be able to see through the false idea of a self.

Reflecting on negative states of mind

The question is, though, will you do that? There is a downside to positive states. When we're feeling positive there is no pressing need to reflect. Our energy is flowing, we're happy, we're not aware of any problems – so what is there to think about? Negative states, on the other hand, are usually painful – our sense of self feels constricted, frustrated, uptight – and this gives us a strong incentive to reflect. What happened? What went wrong? Why am I suffering? How can I stop suffering? Looked at from this point of view, reflecting on – and while in – an intensely negative state, such as anger, jealousy or craving, can be more productive than reflecting when in a positive state. Not that we need to cultivate a negative state in order to provide this opportunity! But we might as well make the most of it when it comes along, as it no doubt will.

When we're in the grip of a negative emotion we seem to experience a very intense and solid self. Negative emotions strengthen the illusion that there's a self doing the experiencing – they are 'self-ish'. As you're reading this book, you've probably forgotten about yourself, but if someone were to come in and shout at you for something you forgot to do, your sense of yourself would probably immediately leap back into consciousness, causing you to feel, say, angry. The Buddha once said that the sense of self is like a barb, 'hard to see, nestling in the heart'.[11] When our needs and wants are satisfied we don't notice its presence. It's only when something or someone interrupts our enjoyment or thwarts our desires that the self becomes conscious.

While negative states may give us a strong incentive to reflect, they also pose quite a big problem: when we're in a negative state we tend to be unreasonable. The more intense the emotion, the more unreasonable we tend to be. Take the example I gave above, of someone interrupting you while you're reading, and shouting at you for forgetting to do something. Let's say that you do react to that interruption by getting angry. That would be understandable, but it wouldn't be reasonable, because there isn't really a valid reason for your anger. If the person who shouted at you is right – you did forget to do something you promised to do – you can simply admit it and apologise. If they are wrong – you did in fact remember to do that thing, or you were unable to do it because of circumstances outside your control, or you never promised to do it in the first place – then you can point that out. But either way, why the anger? Of course, whatever you may or may not have done, they shouldn't have shouted at you, but there still isn't a good reason for you to feel angry. Your accuser may be in a negative state, but why retaliate by getting into a negative state yourself? What purpose might that serve?

Negative emotions tend to be self-justifying. When we're very angry with someone we usually feel that we're quite justified in feeling angry. That's why, when we have a row with someone, we're likely to say some silly things – things that later, when we're in a more reasonable state, we regret having said. This self-justification makes it unlikely that we'll reflect on the anger. We don't feel the need to, because in our view the case is clear: 'He treated me unfairly. He had no right to speak to me that way. I'm perfectly right in feeling angry. I need to put him in his place.' However, it's also the very unreasonableness of such states that makes them potentially rich sources of reflection. If we can bring to them the kind of honest critical awareness that Gabriel Marcel describes, then we might begin to realize how ridiculous we're being. Why such anger? What does it really matter that he shouted at me? So what if he accused me unfairly? Who am I feeling angry for? Who, in fact, is feeling the anger?

Owning up to our foolishness

One of the reasons we find this difficult to do is pride, which is an inflated sense of our own importance. To see the unreasonableness of our position we have to overcome our pride and realize how foolish we're being, and this is humiliating. When I say foolish I don't necessarily mean something really obviously stupid, like succumbing to road rage or falling hopelessly in love with some young beauty who hasn't even noticed that you exist. Foolishness can be quite sophisticated: the consultant surgeon, the CEO of a corporation, the university professor, the famous writer, can all be very foolish too, although their foolishness may be hidden behind a show of expertise and dignity.

A little while ago I decided to reflect on any act of foolishness I might commit. It didn't take long for something to present itself. I had sent an email to someone complaining about a message that he'd sent me, which I thought indicated that he didn't trust me. (I'd happily tell you the content of the message, but it was about a rather technical issue that is a bit too involved to explain easily here.) He replied pointing out something that I'd previously done

The Art of Reflection

which explained why he'd written what he did. And it did explain it. I could see immediately that what he'd written was justified. So I apologized. Of course I wanted to forget the embarrassing and shameful incident – to put it out of sight as soon as possible – but I made myself reflect on it. Why did I do what I did? And why did I send that email, so full of righteous indignation? I realized that I'd been thinking of myself – 'seeing' myself – as a mature and responsible person. It was as if I'd been playing the part of this person, but now my behaviour suddenly seemed ridiculous, like a pompous professor in a farce.

As I reflected on what had happened, I could see that what I'd done wasn't just an isolated incident. I couldn't say that I'd behaved out of character and that what I'd done 'wasn't really me'. I had to admit that it *was* me. Once I'd owned up to my foolishness in that situation I began to see that I was playing the part of this mature, responsible adult in other situations too. Soon I was seeing it everywhere – in almost all my actions and interactions with others. In fact it began to get a bit frightening: just how deeply, utterly foolish was I? Reflecting on this was intensely humiliating and embarrassing – I burned with shame – but it was also exhilarating. I was no longer sure who I was, what I was actually like. It felt as if my 'moorings' had come loose and I was floating free. The mature and responsible persona I'd adopted had given me a sense of security and a touch of superiority, but it had also constrained me. In playing this part I'd had to hold down and even deny what I was really like. In owning up to my foolishness I liberated my natural flow of energy.

Of course, there's a danger in owning up to our foolishness. As we've seen, most people over-estimate their positive qualities, think that they are above average in most areas of life, and tend to interpret events in ways that maintain an image of themselves as being competent, capable, and good. Most people, but not all. Depressed people have a much more accurate view of themselves.[12] They possess what psychologists call 'depressive realism', and while this makes it easy for them to own up to their foolishness, it can also tip them into depression. I have a tendency to depression myself, and while

I was seeing the full extent of my foolishness I was also aware of a temptation to feel very bad about myself. I resisted this because I knew from past experience that self-loathing doesn't lead to self-knowledge or change. It's important to remember that foolishness is not the same as worthlessness. Once again, positive emotions are helpful here. If we can gain our sense of value and well-being from emotional positivity rather than from being competent and capable, we won't mind admitting that sometimes we can be quite foolish. From this perspective it's easy to see how helpful positive emotions can be in human relations. Problems in communication often come down to the fact that someone is unable to admit that they were wrong or that they behaved foolishly, and the reason they are unable to admit it is because the cost to their self-esteem is too high.

Reflecting on suffering

Not all our suffering, though, is caused by our unskilful actions. We also suffer through events outside our control. Someone behaves badly towards us; we become ill; an economic downturn means we can't afford to pay the mortgage; someone we love dies. If you're a Buddhist you'll know that the Buddha taught that all compounded things are, in the final analysis, painful.[13] We may be familiar with this teaching and may have assented to it on a certain level, but when something happens that causes us pain we are often stunned, surprised, even outraged. 'How has this happened? Why has this happened to me? This shouldn't be happening.' It's as if we have a script for our lives that doesn't include anything painful happening to us. Such emotional reactions show us that we haven't yet really understood the Buddha's teaching; we haven't taken it to heart. They show us that what we really believe is that our life should be pleasant, free of difficulties, problems, inconveniences, mess and suffering. As Frank Sinatra sang: 'Oh the good life/ full of fun/ seems to be/ the ideal'. We may even have been practising the Dharma so that we can have this 'good life', so when we do suffer we feel that something has gone wrong – there's been a cosmic mistake!

However, suffering is inevitable as long as we have physical bodies and as long as we have needs and desires. We're susceptible to injury, illness, loss, betrayal, disappointment, grief, death, and a thousand other things. Painful events give us opportunities to understand life more deeply, but only if we reflect on them. If we don't reflect, we can go 'to hell and back', as the tabloid newspapers like to put it, and learn nothing at all. Experience on its own won't teach us anything. We often engage in a kind of inner struggle when we're suffering: we resist the suffering, we fight it, we try to conquer it so that we can go back to the pleasant life we had before the pain began, back to the pleasant life we feel is our birthright. Of course, if we can put things right and alleviate our suffering we should do that, but much of our suffering is not amenable to our will. We can struggle incredibly hard and still fail to overcome it. In fact the struggle adds to our pain. Instead, if we reflect, we might learn something. We can't escape suffering, but we can become wise.

Loss

Everyone suffers loss at some point in their lives: loved ones, money, possessions, youth, health, ability, beauty, trust, love, faith, status, position, power, respect, reputation, and eventually, life. But what *is* loss? Loss implies ownership: we can only lose something that's ours. What does it mean to own something? The answer to this might seem obvious, but let's reflect a little on the question. Across from the desk I'm sitting at is a painting that I bought some time ago; it's 'my' painting. What does that actually mean? It means I can do what I want with it – hang it on a wall wherever I live, sell it, destroy it or give it away. That much is obvious, but what I'm interested in is the effect that owning that painting has on my attitude towards it: that feeling of ownership, that feeling of its being 'mine'. If I came home one day to find that it had been stolen I would feel some pain. A component of that pain would be the prospect of not being able to look at it any more, because I enjoy looking at it, and I would be deprived of that pleasure. However, another component of the pain would be that I would feel *diminished*. I would somehow be less than I was before, as if a part of me had been taken away. On page 46 I quoted a Tibetan definition of ignorance. From the same source comes a definition of greed, which is 'longing desire to possess objects of sensuous cognition which you like, and to include them in your ego-identity, in the hope of getting a sense of security from "having them as part of you".' As I already own the painting, I don't have a 'longing desire to possess' it, but now I'm *attached* to it. If greed is longing desire to *possess* objects etc., then attachment is the desire to *keep* the objects that we possess. So attachment, like greed, is connected with a sense of security. Apparently, the pain we feel on losing something is approximately twice the amount of pleasure we experienced on getting it in the first place![14] Perhaps this is because we become habituated to our circumstances. Before I owned that painting I didn't depend on it for my sense of well-being, but now that I've got used to owning it, I do. Most of the time I'm unaware of this dependency. I don't realize the extent to which owning that painting, along with all the other things I own, is continually contributing to my sense of well-being. It's only when something is stolen or lost or destroyed that I feel bereft – which is to say that I feel diminished and insecure.

So the sense of loss can give us quite a lot to reflect on. What is it? What am I losing, and why does losing it cause me pain?

Of the things that can be lost which I listed above, some are tangible – loved ones, money, possessions, health – and the loss of them would make a tangible difference to our lives. Other things we can lose are intangible: status, position, respect, and reputation. They are to do with how people see us, or think about us. Or perhaps, more accurately, they are to do with how *we think* other people see us. If we were to lose our status or reputation, what real difference would that make to our lives? We would still have the same amount of money and possessions, we would continue to live in the same home, our family and friends would all be intact, and we wouldn't go hungry. (Of course in some instances a loss of reputation might also entail a loss of one's livelihood, which would make a tangible difference to one's life, but it would be the loss of livelihood that made the tangible difference, not the loss of reputation in itself.)

There's no doubt that when we lose our reputation, for instance, we feel pain; we feel diminished by the loss. But what have we actually lost? We're more or less the same person today, now that we've lost our reputation, as we were yesterday, before we lost it. We still possess the same number of virtues and vices, strengths and weaknesses. Of course people will think differently about us today, now that we have lost our reputation, than they did yesterday, when our reputation was intact, so we've lost other people's good opinion of us. But if they had a good opinion of us yesterday and a bad opinion of us today, even though we are the same person today as we were yesterday, of what value is their opinion? Either they were wrong yesterday or they are wrong today. Perhaps their ideas about us were inaccurate on both days! So does it really matter? We are as we are, no matter what other people think about us.

Well, perhaps it shouldn't matter, but it does, and this is because the way we think and feel about ourselves is very often dependent on the way others think and feel about us. If others think badly of us it's difficult not to feel badly about ourselves, even though their opinion of us may be based on mistaken information, or on values that we don't share with them. We're social animals with a very strong need to feel accepted and to belong. The loss of reputation, status, position etc. is *felt* as a loss because we feel that we're losing our place in the society to which we belong. So when people speak badly of us, or an unpleasant rumour about us is being spread, or we're accused of something that we didn't do, we have a good opportunity for reflection. Is there any truth in what they are saying about me? If so, what can I do about that – how can I change? If there's no truth in what they say, why am I upset by it? Why is my feeling of well-being dependent on other people's opinion of me?

Grief

Losing things hurts. Some losses are quite small and the hurt we feel is correspondingly small – a favourite cup breaks, we receive a parking fine, a thief steals our wallet. Sometimes our losses are great. When we lose something of great value to us, or someone we love deeply, we feel grief – the pain of separation. When we suffer great loss, all we can do is live with it, day after day, letting its pain teach us that life is short, everything in this world is impermanent, and there is nothing we can do about it.

Part of my work is to run courses in mindfulness and meditation for people with chronic pain and other long-term health conditions – conditions that cannot be cured. Mindfulness and meditation help them to live well with their pain or other unpleasant symptoms. The direct physical symptoms of their conditions aren't the only cause of their suffering, though. They have also experienced tremendous loss: loss of health, of course, but also in many cases, their career, or at least livelihood, and therefore income; their social life; sometimes their partner, who feels unable to cope with the demands of living with someone with a serious health condition; the ability to play with their children; social standing, and many other losses. Telling them that their grief is due to attachment is not going to help them very much. What does help is if they can learn to be with their loss in an openhearted way, rather than trying to avoid, deny or harden against their grief. We even suggest that they 'move towards' their suffering with a sense of kindness, gentleness, and compassion. This can be transformative. Rather than making them more unhappy, as some people might imagine, learning to be with their suffering allows them also to experience joy, beauty and love.

The poet Naomi Shihab Nye wrote that:

> Before you know what kindness really is
> you must lose things,
> feel the future dissolve in a moment
> like salt in a weakened broth.
> What you held in your hand,
> what you counted and carefully saved,
> all this must go so you know
> how desolate the landscape can be
> between the regions of kindness.[15]

The Art of Reflection

Of course loss doesn't necessarily bring about kindness. It can, instead, make us bitter and resentful. Whether loss makes us kinder or not depends largely on how we approach it.

> Before you know kindness as the deepest thing inside,
> you must know sorrow as the other deepest thing.
> You must wake up with sorrow.
> You must speak to it till your voice
> catches the thread of all sorrows
> and you see the size of the cloth.

What is the size of the cloth? As big as the world. If we allow ourselves to experience our loss fully, with a kind, tender heart, we begin to realize that it is part of the human condition, and this insight connects us with the whole of life.

Chapter Three

....

Dwelling on a Topic

You do not need to leave your room. Remain sitting at your table and listen. Do not even listen, simply wait. Do not even wait, be quite still and solitary. The world will freely offer itself to you to be unmasked, it has no choice, it will roll in ecstasy at your feet.[1]

Franz Kafka

There is one skill that's indispensable for reflection: the ability to keep your mind on a subject over a sustained period of time. The mind has a natural tendency to wander, and although wandering can be fun, and we can sometimes find ourselves in some interesting places on our travels, we need to learn to stay put sometimes. Much of our wandering is motivated by boredom, by the need to find something new, different, novel, exciting. It's easy to give in to the temptation to move on to something new, but if we do that all the time we'll never get to know a subject well. We'll know a little about many things, but we won't know anything very deeply. We need to learn to dwell in one place for a while, to see things that we didn't notice at first, to enter some of the buildings we've only seen from the outside.

In Chapter 1 I wrote about *vitakka* and *vicāra*: initial thought and sustained thought. You may remember that initial thought is your mind first alighting on a subject, while sustained thought is staying with the subject over a period of time. I recently read a beautiful metaphor that describes the difference between the two. Initial thought is like a hammer hitting a bell, causing it to ring out. Sustained thought is like the continuous reverberation of the bell – the sustained note. Of course, eventually the note dies away, but the better the quality of the bell, the longer the note will carry on. We need to become like a high-quality bell. The mindfulness of breathing meditation really helps because in this practice we dwell on the breath, bringing our mind back whenever it wanders. But we can choose any object to practise on, anything at all. Look at an object – your hand, a flower, a dustbin – for ten minutes at a time to begin with. Or listen to the sounds around you.

A key to paying attention is interest. If we're interested in something we'll be able to sustain our attention more easily. Heidegger tells us that the word interest comes from the Latin word *interesse*, which means 'to be among and in the midst of things, or to be at the centre of a thing and to stay with it'.[2] If you think your ability to pay attention is poor, think of a time when you last enjoyed watching a film, reading a novel, playing a sport, gardening, or something else you enjoy doing. Your mind probably didn't wander very much, if at all. We easily become absorbed when we're doing something we enjoy. So find something you're interested in and pay attention to that.

However, it can work the other way round too. Things tend to become more interesting as we pay attention to them. We've all seen countless trees, chairs, cars and houses, and we've heard the wind, birdsong, trains, footsteps, so many times that we no longer really look or listen. We see a cup, for instance, but we don't really notice its particular shape, its colour, the way the light falls onto it so that part of it is shaded, the way it reflects some of the other objects around it, showing distorted pictures of them. A cup can be fascinating. So can the sound of a dog barking in the distance, or the smell of smoke, or the texture of a dishcloth. This evening, after I'd finished eating my dinner, I noticed the dishcloth that I'd carelessly draped over the kitchen tap. It is a light blue, but when I noticed it, it was darker in places, where it was still wet. I gazed at it for a while. It was quite beautiful. I don't mean that it was pretty, but it seemed so real, so present, so textured, as if a really good painter – say Vermeer – had painted it. Of course Vermeer didn't paint dishcloths, but if he had, I think it might have looked something like this one.

Buddhism considers the mind to be another sense – the sixth sense. Just as we can look at, or listen to, or feel the texture of an object, we can also hold an object in the mind. A memory, an image, an idea, a problem that needs to be solved: these are all 'mind objects'. If you can learn how to pay attention to your breath or a cup, then you can do the same with a mind object. I want to suggest a few ways that can help us to dwell on a subject, to live with it for a while – to get to know it better.

Talking to yourself

In his book *Philosophy as a Way of Life* Pierre Hadot writes about the practice of what he calls 'inner dialogue':

> Meditation – the practice of dialogue with oneself – seems to have held a place of honour amongst Socrates' disciples. When Antisthenes was asked what profit he had derived from philosophy, he replied 'The ability to converse with myself'.[3]

That's a good way of thinking of reflection: having a conversation with yourself. This could be in the form of questions and answers. Asking ourselves questions can help us to penetrate into a subject more deeply – just keep on asking questions, giving answers, and then asking questions of those answers. For instance, you might be thinking about the Threefold Way of ethics, meditation, and wisdom, and you might ask yourself why, or how, the practice of ethics helps us to concentrate. Here's how the conversation might go:

> Answer: 'Concentration' here is a translation of *samādhi*, which is better translated as absorption, or even wholeness or integration. So the practice of ethics helps us to become integrated or whole.
>
> Question: What does that mean?

The Art of Reflection

A: An integrated mind is one in which all the parts are harmonized, or leading in the same direction. An unintegrated mind is one that wants incompatible things, so there is conflict.

Q: Yes, but that's very abstract. What does it mean in concrete terms?

A: Hmm, let's think of an example. Someone might want to devote themselves to living the spiritual life, but they might be susceptible to outbreaks of anger, and that tendency goes counter to everything else they value. The anger is therefore an unintegrated aspect of their life.

Q: OK, but how does that person integrate that anger into their life?

A: It's not that they integrate the anger into their life, it's more that they need to somehow liberate the energy that expresses itself in anger, and express that energy in a more skilful way.

Q: For instance?

A: They might take up some kind of sport, which allows them to channel that energy into something harmless. Then they won't feel the need to express anger in other situations.

Q: But now you're saying that taking up sport is conducive to *samādhi* or absorption, so it's not just ethics that we need to practise.

A: Well, I was just giving the example of someone who was prone to outbursts of anger, and saying that taking up a sport might help them practise ethics, which includes the non-expression of anger.

Q: But does the channelling of their energy into that sport really mean that they're integrating it into their life? Aren't they diverting their energy into sport, rather than integrating it?

Obviously that conversation can go much further and deeper, and perhaps throws up more questions than it answers, but I'm not going to waste your time by telling you how *I* might think it through. After all, I'm writing this book to encourage *you* to reflect. This is just an example of how you might reflect by asking yourself questions, following the argument through, trying not to get distracted from your main theme.

Another kind of conversation you might have is to take two sides of an argument and argue for both. This can be very helpful if you're not sure what you think or what you should do. For it to be effective you have to really argue for both sides, as if you really mean it. Let's say a good friend has moved to live abroad and they've invited you to visit them for a couple of weeks. You'd love to do that but you'd have to go by plane – it would take a week to get there by ship – and you're aware that travelling by air is ethically questionable. Now you're not sure what to do. You have an 'ethical dilemma'. Here's how you might argue for and against:

> *For:* My friendship is very valuable to me, so I think the benefits of visiting my friend outweigh the ecological effects of flying.

> *Against*: Everyone thinks that of their own situation, and everyone continues to fly. Meanwhile we're heading for a global catastrophe.

> *For:* Assuming that those scientists are right who argue that we're responsible for global warming. Not all scientists agree.

> *Against:* True, but the majority do, and while we can't be 100% certain we should assume that it is the case.

> *For*: OK, but I don't think my situation is the same as that of everyone else who flies. Many people go on holiday abroad when they could have a holiday in their own country, or travel by train or ship.

The Art of Reflection

Against: That may be true, but I expect most people who fly will have their own good reasons – they're called rationalizations!

For: Actually I don't think I'm rationalizing. Friendship is important, and this friend is very important to me.

Against: OK. It's important. What we're trying to do is weigh up the importance of visiting her against the probable negative effects of flying. Can you justify it? How about setting up a Skype connection? Wouldn't that do?

For: I can do that, but I don't think that's a substitute for actually being with her. Perhaps I can plant a tree to offset the effects.

Against: Mmm, dubious. A sop to your conscience.

Again, the argument can go a lot further than this – I've only stopped here because my intention is just to give an example of how you might argue for and against something. And it's not meant to be an example of a perfectly logical argument. We're trying to clarify our thoughts about something, and during the course of our clarification of course some of our thinking will be a bit muddled, and we'll tend to rationalize our desires and make non-sequiturs – that is, inferences or conclusions that don't follow from the premises. If we continue to reflect as honestly as we can, gradually we'll begin to understand the issue better.

Hadot writes that:

> The same thing happens in every spiritual exercise: we must *let* ourselves be changed, in our point of view, attitudes, and convictions. This means that we must dialogue with ourselves, and hence we must do battle with ourselves.[4]

To think something through in this way requires great honesty and courage, because if we follow reason we might find ourselves coming to a conclusion that we'd rather not come to, a conclusion that tells us we can't have what we want. I referred to the problem above as an ethical dilemma, but I remember a friend once telling me that he thought there were very few genuine ethical dilemmas. The conflict we usually have is not between two equally ethical options, but rather between the more ethical option, which we don't want to do, and the less ethical option, which we do want to do. Reflection will often make this clear to us. The choice is still ours, but we may have to admit that the choice we make is sometimes the less ethical one.

Reflective writing

One way of keeping one's mind on a topic is to write about it. Someone once asked my teacher, Sangharakshita, how they could learn to think. He suggested that they write about the same topic every day for half an hour. A few years ago, I decided to try this out, over a period of two months. On the first day I wrote down everything I already knew about the subject – that is, everything I'd learned from others. The second day was more difficult because now I had to write down my own thoughts. I sat there for some time, bringing my mind back whenever it wandered off, fighting with the urge to do something else and trying to ignore the little voice saying 'This is a waste of time.' However, I did manage to write something, and this felt like a small victory, because it was my own! 'Hey, it's possible to have an original thought if I sit here long enough!' As the days went by, sometimes I sat there at a loss, not having anything to write about at all, but on other days it was as if the floodgates opened and I wrote pages, sometimes going on for well over an hour.

Writing can help the process of reflection because when you write down your thoughts, you 'objectify' them. There they are, on the page, so you can always refer back to them, whereas if you are just sitting down to think, your thoughts can be a little elusive – 'What was that thought I just had? How did it relate to what I was thinking earlier? What *was* I thinking earlier?' Also, a thought that seemed significant while it was in your mind can look a little naïve when seen on the page. You can also review your writing later and decide which thoughts may be worth pondering further, and which you can discard.

There's a second phase in this process if you want to try it: write an essay or give a talk. This will mean putting your thoughts into some kind of shape, ordering them so that they make a coherent argument. This is quite different from the first phase, which consists in having new, perhaps startling thoughts about something. The first phase can be very creative and exciting, if a little chaotic. The second phase consists in testing these ideas out and seeing if they really make sense, if they are coherent, if they make sense to someone else. It's often in this phase that you begin to see the flaws in your thinking, the faulty logic, the guesswork, the connections that don't quite connect. Francis Bacon wrote that 'reading maketh a full man; conference a ready man; and writing an exact man.'[5] As I mentioned in the Introduction, many times during the writing of this book I've been forced to stop and re-think a sentence or a paragraph, knowing that it didn't really work. It didn't work because it wasn't quite true. Often an idea that sounds good in my own mind, or mentioned over breakfast, will not pass the writing test.

This second phase isn't just one of criticism and tidying up; it's also part of the creative process. When I begin writing, say a chapter of this book, I think that I know what I want to say, and that all I have to do is write it out. But in the writing I realize that I don't know what I want to say because I'm not sure yet exactly what I think. I realize that my thoughts are still vague, imprecise, shallow, unsubstantiated. They mean well but they're unconvincing. Writing helps you to take your thinking further and deeper and truer. It helps you to think more exactly so that you can say exactly what you mean. As Mark Tredinnick writes in his book *Writing Well*:

> A sentence makes the meaning it makes out of the
> process of its own unravelling. Out of a process itself
> chaotic – the thinking of thoughts and the embarkation
> upon one's sentences – a writer discovers what it is
> she's really trying to say and how she needs to hang it
> together.[6]

Thinking with your legs

Walking is good too. Many well-known thinkers recommend it as an aid to thinking. Jean-Jacques Rousseau wrote, 'I can only meditate when I'm walking. When I stop, my mind ceases to think; my mind only works with my legs.'[7] I'm a late convert to walking as a way of reflecting. I've always been a sit-down thinker, but in the interests of research for this book I recently tried it out. I had very good conditions. I was on a three-week solitary retreat and there was something I needed to think through: I had to give a talk at a convention a few days after my retreat, on a topic that was very important to me. The weather was good so I went for a fairly long walk every day. I was delighted to find that every day I'd return to my hut with one or two new thoughts about my subject. I felt like a hunter returning every day with a catch, and I think there was only one day when I came back empty-handed. It was as if the act of walking out in the fresh air dislodged ideas that had been jammed up, and my thinking would develop with each walk. I'd be very pleased with an idea one day, and the next day I'd see that it was flawed, or that it wasn't finished, or that it wasn't true in every situation, or that a metaphor I'd used didn't quite tell the whole truth.

Reflecting with others

So far in this book I've been discussing reflection as a solitary activity, something best done alone, but it's also possible to reflect with others. A few years ago I lived and worked in a Buddhist study centre, and as part of my work I led many study seminars. Sometimes I ran seminars for people who had as much knowledge and experience as I did, and this made me think about my role as a 'teacher'. I couldn't 'teach' these people, so what should I be doing? I came to the conclusion that in these situations my function was not to teach in the sense of sharing my knowledge and experience, but to try to create a context in which we could all learn together. That entailed co-creating an atmosphere of trust, out of which we might be able to reflect collectively.

Much of the time we spent in discussion we were *not* reflecting collectively: we were swapping information, showing off our knowledge, listening to each other with half an ear while thinking of a reply, getting annoyed when someone disagreed with one of our considered opinions, and talking far too much. In other words, we spent a lot of time collectively *papañcizing*. Occasionally, though, we would enter a quiet, thoughtful space together, and it was like suddenly coming to a clearing in the midst of a thick forest. These were wonderful moments, in which we all seemed to be reflecting on a topic together. We would all be listening intently to one another, thoughtfully considering what others said, no longer eager to put forward our own particular point of view, and only speaking if we really had something to say that would further our collective enquiry. I learned so much at those times.

Some of my friends and I have been experimenting recently with different ways of reflecting with others. One of these ways I call 'reflecting out loud'. This can be done with a group of people or with just one other, but for ease of explanation I'll describe how it's done with just one other. First choose what you are going to reflect on – it can be a Buddhist teaching, a line or a verse from a text, something from your own experience, anything. Then decide who will be the first to reflect and who will be the listener. Let's say it's you who begins. Tell your partner what you are going to reflect on, and if it's a verse or a line from a text, recite that verse or line. Then begin reflecting 'out loud' – that is, speaking whatever thoughts arise in relation to the topic. Don't worry if there are pauses in between your thoughts – that's natural, and there may be more silence than speaking. Don't feel under pressure to keep talking to entertain your partner. Feel free to remain silent for minutes on end.

The listener doesn't need to do anything other than listen attentively. However, before you begin reflecting you can tell your partner if you are happy for them to help you in some way, if it seems appropriate. Ways of helping might include suggesting that you have strayed a little off the topic, asking what some of the implications might be of something you've just said, or asking how you feel about something you've said. The listener needs to be very sensitive about how much they say. People want to be helpful, and this sometimes results in them saying too much, intruding on the natural flow of your reflections. If you feel they are doing this you need to ask them gently to say less.

Once you have reflected in this way for some time – you can start with 15 minutes – then you swap roles.

Nearly everyone I've introduced this to has found it very effective, because, as with writing, when you say a thought out loud it becomes more objective. It's a good way to stay with a topic too, because there is a gentle pressure to stick with it when someone else is listening.[8]

Everyone reflects in their own way

I've just suggested four ways in which you might develop your capacity to dwell on a topic – inner dialogue, writing, walking, and reflecting with others – but there are many other ways to think. In his book *Poetry in the Making*, Ted Hughes has a chapter called 'Learning to Think', in which he writes:

> One of the odd wonderful things about this activity we call thinking is that to some extent everybody invents their own brand, has his own way of thinking, not only his own thoughts. You do not ever have to worry that you are not thinking properly . . . all you have to do really is think. And thinking, as we know, is as natural as breathing – some sort of thinking is generally going on in us all the time. So what is all the fuss about?[9]

So we just have to do it, in whatever way comes naturally to us. Don't worry if your thinking seems to be chaotic, undisciplined, and untidy. In my experience that's how it often is – more like a wild habitat than an English garden. If you stay with your topic for long enough your thinking will distil into one or two thoughts worthy of the name. Sometimes they will crystallize into a question. It's as if all your random, chaotic thinking has thrown up the question you need to answer, even though you were not previously aware that there was a question that needed an answer.

A good question is worth many hours of chaotic thinking. We tend to value answers more than questions. We think of questions as means to an end – it's answers that we really want – but good questions are immensely valuable. In fact reflection thrives on questions, much more so than answers. If you had all the answers, why would you need to reflect?

Reflection is a deepening of the self

So far I've been discussing reflection as conscious thought: choose a topic and think about it. But not all reflection consists in deliberately thinking about issues that are available to our conscious minds. There may seem not to be very much in your conscious mind at all. You may be aware that there is 'something there' – something to be got at, a feeling, an intuition – but you don't know what it is. You find that out later. Here's Ted Hughes again:

> There is the inner life, which is the world of final reality,
> the world of memory, emotion, imagination, intelligence,
> and natural common sense, and which goes on all the
> time, consciously or unconsciously, like the heart beat.
> There is also the thinking process by which we break
> into that inner life and capture answers and evidence
> to support the answers out of it. That process of raid, or
> persuasion, or ambush, or dogged hunting, or surrender,
> is the kind of thinking we have to learn and if we do not
> somehow learn it, then our minds lie in us like the fish in
> a pond of a man who cannot fish.[10]

Hughes uses quite active, even violent metaphors in this passage – 'break into . . . capture . . . raid . . . ambush' – but a little later he expands on the fishing metaphor, and shows that the process is gentler, more receptive:

> As you know, all a fisherman does is stare at his float
> for hours on end. I have spent hundreds and hundreds
> of hours staring at a float – a dot of red or yellow the

size of a lentil, ten yards away. Those of you who have never done it, might think it is a very drowsy pastime. It is anything but that. All the little nagging impulses, that are normally distracting your mind, dissolve. They have to dissolve if you are to go on fishing. If they do not, then you cannot settle down: you get bored and pack up in a bad temper. But once they have dissolved, you enter one of the orders of bliss.

Your whole being rests lightly on your float, but not drowsily: very alert, so that the least twitch of the float arrives like an electric shock. And you are not only watching the float. You are aware, in a horizonless and slightly mesmerized way, like listening to the double bass in orchestral music, of the fish below there in the dark. At every moment your imagination is alarming itself with the size of the thing slowly leaving the weeds and approaching your bait. Or with the world of beauties down there, suspended in total ignorance of you. And the whole purpose of this concentrated excitement, in this arena of apprehension and unforeseeable events, is to bring up some lovely solid thing like living metal from a world where nothing exists but those inevitable facts which raise life out of nothing and return it to nothing.

So you see, fishing with a float is a sort of mental exercise in concentration on a small point, while at the same time letting your imagination work freely to collect everything that might concern that still point: in this case the still point is the float and the things that concern the float are all the fish you are busy imagining.

Reflection then is not merely a mental exercise in ideas; it is also an enlargement of self-awareness. We might begin to reflect on a topic so that we understand *it* more deeply, but this process involves understanding *ourselves* more deeply. Often the reason we have a relatively shallow understanding of something is not because we lack information, but because *we* are relatively shallow. The person we are at the moment is incapable of a deeper understanding. Our understanding deepens as we deepen.

In Chapter 2 I mentioned Alexander McCall Smith's Isabel Dalhousie novels as good examples of reflection. Delightful as these novels are, they are quite light-hearted and perhaps don't go very deep. I recently read another reflective novel – Marilynne Robinson's *Gilead* – which is more serious and penetrates a little deeper. In this novel John Ames is an aged pastor who knows he hasn't got much longer to live. He has a young son who will not have the opportunity to grow up with his father, so John decides to write a long letter to him, or a series of letters, to be read when he's older. The letters consist of John's reflections, partly on his life – things that have happened, things that he's done – and partly on matters of Christian doctrine. Here he is reflecting on grief:

> My custom has always been to ponder grief; that is,
> to follow it through ventricle and aorta to find out its
> lurking places. That old weight on the chest, telling me
> there is something I must dwell on, because I know more
> than I know and must learn it from myself.[11]

'I know more than I know and must learn it from myself.' What a wonderful line that is. When we reflect, we're our own teacher, and one of the ways we teach ourselves is by bringing into consciousness something that we already, at some less conscious level, know. Recently I was leading a workshop on reflection and I asked everyone to sit and write for 45 minutes. I decided to write about my love of solitude to try to understand better why it's so important to me. At one point I looked out of the window for a few minutes, resting my eyes on a hill covered with pine and larch trees, and a question spontaneously arose in my mind: Why don't I love my life more than I do? This was a completely unexpected question, but it felt as if it was the very thing that I needed to dwell on. It was as if my first choice of topic was merely a way into this deeper question. And there isn't a simple answer, such as 'I need to get married' or 'I need a new job'. The question challenges something deeper inside me, something about me or my life that I haven't yet understood – something that I need to learn from myself.

The pleasure of reflection

Recently I reflected on *how* I reflect. I realized as I was writing this book that I didn't know how I did it, so I spent some time observing myself, and this is what I discovered. First I sit down and allow my being to settle. I compose myself. I become aware of my body and its various sensations, because I think best when the whole of myself is included. I look down at my feet; I feel the contact of my feet on the floor. I feel my stomach rise and fall with the breath. I need time: an open expanse of time spreading out ahead of me, so that I don't feel rushed. To rush is to constrain, and I need to feel that I have time for my mind to expand, time in which I can unfurl and explore. There is a delicious pleasure in idleness, in not doing anything useful, in playing.

Then I just wait. At first there may be no thoughts at all. If I have a problem that I've been trying to solve, I'll remind myself of it. I'll notice the feeling the problem evokes in me: interest, perplexity, discomfort, annoyance, insecurity. Or perhaps I don't have a problem or a question to answer. Perhaps I just want to know a subject better. Then it's as if I'm standing outside a walled garden that I want to enter: to see, feel and smell the plants, trees, grass and earth. Or it's as if I'm looking at an intricate mechanism like a watch, and want to prise the back off and see how it works. This kind of reflecting has no function or use. No immediate use, anyway. I'm thinking for the simple pleasure of thinking, of considering something, of getting to know the world I inhabit better. Sometimes there is no particular topic I want to think about and so I just wait and see what presents itself to me. There is usually something sitting just below my conscious mind that needs attending to, some unresolved issue or source of unhappiness that just needs a little gentle coaxing into consciousness.

This leads me to another point – something that surprised me when I noticed it. I don't actually 'think', in the sense that I *do* something. I can't make thinking happen. Instead, I allow thoughts to arise. I bring a subject to mind, and then I wait. Perhaps the majority of the time my mind is empty. I'm just waiting for thoughts to appear. Thoughts arise or they don't. There's a sense of letting thoughts come to me, rather than my having thoughts or bringing them into existence. Sometimes stray, random thoughts appear: I remember that I have to phone someone, or that we've run out of cornflakes. I might write these down to remind myself to see to them later – this frees my mind to continue my reflection.

However, when a thought occurs to me that seems worth following I then exert a gentle effort to stay with it. Just the right amount of effort needed to dwell on that thought to see where it might lead me – I don't need to do any more than that. It's a little like being in a boat being taken along with the current. I don't need to row, I just need to adjust the rudder, gently changing direction every now and then, bringing myself back to the topic.

After a while an idea may come to me that seems new and significant, something I've never thought before, and can't remember reading or hearing from anyone else. This new thought is always accompanied by a rush of excitement and pleasure. I think it may be a similar experience to the creative process of the poet, composer or painter, although I'm not a creative artist so I can't be sure about that. Certainly the experience is of giving birth to something new and fresh. At times like this it feels as if I am learning something, but not in the sense of adding to my stock of information. It's more that I'm seeing the world in a new way, and to do that I've had to become a different person.

The pleasure I get from reflection is not a lazy kind of pleasure, easily obtained, such as I might get from watching a DVD or sitting in the sun. It's the kind of pleasure you get when you are learning a new skill and you can suddenly do something you couldn't do before: that feeling of having stretched yourself, gone beyond your normal boundaries. Marilynne Robinson puts it very well when she has John Ames say:

> I have wandered to the limits of my understanding any number of times . . . and I've scared myself too, a good many times, leaving all landmarks behind me, or so it seemed. And it has been among the true pleasures of my life. Night and light, silence and difficulty, it seemed to me always rigorous and good.[12]

Chapter Four

....

Reading Reflectively

Information is endlessly available to us: where shall wisdom be found?[1]

Harold Bloom

In Peter Ackroyd's novel *The Plato Papers*, set 2,000 years into the future, the novel's protagonist, Plato, looking back at our time, says of us:

> I soon discovered that they always wished to
> communicate in the shortest possible time, the most
> simple piece of information seemed to amuse them,
> as long as it could be gathered instantaneously. . .
> the faster an action could be reported, the more
> significance it acquired. Events themselves were not
> of any consequence, only the fact that they could be
> known quickly. Now you are silent. . . how could I have
> invented such a reality? [2]

This seems an accurate description of our age. With 24-hour news channels, we get to hear about, and often see, events that are happening all over the world as they are happening, or at least very soon afterwards, and the internet gives us instant access to information at the push of a few keys. All this instantaneous communication encourages us to read quickly and makes us impatient and greedy for more.

In this chapter we are going to explore another way of reading that requires a very different attitude: one of quiet, patient and careful consideration. In this way of reading, we might dwell on one page, or even a line, for a few hours, rather than hurrying on to the next page. There is a certain renunciation involved in this because while we're dwelling on just a few words we're not taking in any new information. We may need to give up our thirst for new knowledge, new 'data', and give ourselves instead to the slow, painstaking task of understanding something more deeply. Of course, this way of reading is not appropriate for every kind of reading matter: magazines, blogs and thrillers don't usually require such close and careful attention. A poem, however, or a thoughtful novel, or a philosophical essay, or a religious text, often contains more meaning than we are able to appreciate at first glance. To understand it we need to come into a deeper relationship with it, and to do that we need to give it our full and undivided attention for a while.

> We have forgotten how to read: how to pause, liberate ourselves from our worries, return into ourselves, and leave aside our search for subtlety and originality, in order to meditate calmly, ruminate, and let the texts speak to us. This, too, is a spiritual exercise, and one of the most difficult.[3]

This passage is from a book called *Philosophy as a Way of Life* by Pierre Hadot. He is referring here to ancient Greek and Roman texts, but the same principle applies to any literature that tries to communicate some deeper wisdom. Ours is a very literate culture in which the written word is ubiquitous, from newspapers to internet sites to advertising hoardings to lists of ingredients in packaged food – we can even read our cornflakes packet at breakfast! The benefits of being able to read are enormous, of course, but there is a downside: we can get into the habit of reading for information or entertainment only, and neglect reading to obtain wisdom. This is a very different kind of reading; one that Hadot says is one of the most difficult of spiritual exercises.

Slow reading

The first thing we have to learn is to read slowly, the opposite to speed reading, where you try to read as many words as possible in the shortest time. Speed reading has been invented to help people who, either in their work or in their studies, have to read and take in an enormous amount of information every day. There is now a World Championship Speed Reading Competition, in which the top contestants typically read around 1,000 to 2,000 words per minute with approximately 50% comprehension.[4] According to the *Guinness Book of Records*, the fastest reader in the world, Howard Berg, gets through 25,000 words per minute, with apparently perfect recall. This is obviously a remarkable skill and extremely useful for gathering information, but information is not the same as wisdom. To gain wisdom from a book you need to learn to read slowly. It may seem odd that I'm saying that we should *learn* to read slowly, because you might think that would be an easy thing to do. Actually it isn't, for the simple reason that once you've become used to doing anything quickly it becomes difficult to do slowly – we become habituated to speed. A little while ago I read in a magazine that driving a car at 50 rather than 70 mph uses about 15% less fuel, thereby saving money and also, more importantly, reducing carbon emissions. The next time I drove on a motorway I tried to limit my speed to 50 mph, and it was very, very difficult! My speedometer kept drifting up to 60 – how did that happen?

Friedrich Nietzsche wrote that he was 'a teacher of slow reading', and went on to say:

> In the midst of an age of 'work', that is to say, of hurry, of indecent and perspiring haste, which wants to 'get everything done' at once, including every old or new book:- this art does not so easily get anything done, it teaches to read well, that is to say, to read slowly, deeply, looking cautiously before and aft, with reservations, with doors left open, with delicate eyes and fingers . . .[5]

Let's dwell on this passage for a while and reflect on it, clause by clause, as I'm sure Nietzsche would have liked us to do. *This art does not so easily get anything done.* We can bring our sense of hurry, our attitude of wanting to 'get things done', even to our reading, so that we tally up how many books we've read recently, and if a book takes longer to read than we expected, we become frustrated, because there are other books we want to get on to. We may want to be 'well read', which often means that we've read a lot of books but understood them only superficially. Perhaps we can change the meaning of this phrase so that well read could also mean to have read one book carefully, thoroughly, deeply.

Read slowly means to read carefully, making sure that we understand the meaning of each word and sentence. It's useful to have a dictionary at hand to make sure we know what each word means. Sometimes I can have a vague sense of what a word means, but if I look it up in a dictionary I discover that it means something a little different, and that difference can subtly change the meaning of the passage I'm reading. We should try to understand what the author of the text is saying, rather than making our own interpretations too quickly. When we read a text we're coming into contact with another mind. In a way we're trying to enter the mind of the author, to see the world from his or her point of view. In reflective reading we're using our powers of reflection to *imagine* a different way, someone else's way, of seeing the world.

Deeply means digging below the surface meaning of the text, pausing and reflecting on what we've just read. One way of doing this is to ask questions, such as: Is this true? In all situations? Does this accord with my experience? What implications might this have for me? Do I need to change my life in any way in the light of what I've just read? It may also mean allowing the text to affect us, so that we don't just understand with our intellect but also *feel* the meaning, allowing it to percolate down through deeper layers of our being and letting ourselves be changed. In his book *The Compassionate Mind*, the psychologist Paul Gilbert writes: 'How prepared we are *to allow* ourselves to be emotionally moved can be crucial to how we understand things.'[6] For instance, take the well-known story of Kisa Gotami and the mustard seed, where the young woman Kisa Gotami goes to the Buddha, distraught, holding her dead baby in her arms, and asks him to bring the baby back to life. The Buddha agrees to do this on one condition: that she brings to him a mustard seed from a house where no-one has died. She goes knocking on the door of every house in the town and returns a few hours later, without her dead baby and also without the mustard seed. Of course, in every house she visited there has been a death. As she has gone from door to door, hearing about the deaths in each and every household, she has slowly come to terms with the death of her baby, and when she returns to the Buddha she asks to go for refuge to the Three Jewels. (This is a traditional way of saying that she asks the Buddha to accept her as a disciple and commits her life to practising his teachings.) I expect you know the story – you've probably heard it many times and understand its meaning. However, just imagine if you were really to put yourself in Kisa Gotami's shoes, to feel the pain she felt, the disbelief, the despair. Suppose you really imagined going from house to house, hearing each householder's story, and slowly beginning to accept the fact of the death of your own dearly cherished child. If you felt so much for that woman that you were moved to tears, you'd understand the story differently, wouldn't you?

Looking cautiously before and aft: we need to be aware of the context of each word and sentence, being sensitive to the fact that words can change subtly according to the context. It could also mean that we review our past and imagine our future in the light of what we're reading. You might, for example, read a poem about the brevity of life and understand with more clarity than usual that you really are going to die some day soon. This thought might then set you reflecting on your past: What has it amounted to? Where has it been heading? But you may also find yourself reflecting on your future: What will I do with my remaining time? What's important to me?

With reservations: this could mean that we need to hold back our full assent for the time being, reserving judgement. However, *with doors left open* suggests that we also need to hold ourselves open to the text – we need to be empathic. According to Paul Gilbert, empathy 'consists of both an emotional component and the ability to "understand" . . . Empathy begins with an open-minded curiosity and a genuine desire to know and discover.'[7] So Nietzsche seems to be asking us to do two opposing things at once:

to hold ourselves back at the same time as holding ourselves open. I'm reminded of the poet Keats's 'negative capability', which he described as being a state of 'being in uncertainties, Mysteries, doubts, without any irritable reaching after fact & reason'. I think of it as a state of positive bewilderment in which I have let go of some old opinions but have not yet managed to grasp any new ones. This is an uncomfortable state to be in, and slightly scary, so we often try to bring it to a conclusion prematurely, but it's better if we can stay with the discomfort, as this is the key to the learning process.

Finally, *with delicate eyes and fingers* suggests great care and sensitivity, feeling the different nuances of a phrase, intuiting the meaning behind the words on the page. It even suggests that we treat the physical book in our hands with great care, turning the pages with mindfulness and sensitivity.

When we read in this way we are rather like translators, bringing out the meaning of a text word by word.

> We go unwinding the woof
> from the web of meaning
>
> Words of the Sutras
> day by day come forth
>
> Head on, we chase the mystery of the Dharma.[8]

Reading traditional Buddhist texts

This approach to reading can illuminate all manner of texts, bringing to light the truth that is in them – or sometimes exposing a lack of depth or truth. If you're a Buddhist I'd like to encourage you to read a few traditional Buddhist texts, that is, those attributed to the Buddha or some of the other great teachers of the past. The Buddhist tradition has a really vast body of literature, all of which has been written to help us to understand the causes of our suffering and to enable us to become wiser, kinder, more generous, more aware, more compassionate – in other words, to gain Enlightenment. So it's well worth reading! And as you can read English, you are very lucky, because much of it has been translated into English. You can even read a lot for free on the internet. If you are aligned to a particular school of Buddhism, you may want to read some of the books considered important by that school. If you are not so aligned, you have the whole Buddhist tradition to choose from. This in itself can pose a problem though: you may feel a little daunted by the vast amount of material now available in translation. Where to start?

I would recommend that you begin with the teachings of the Buddha himself, as found in the Pali canon. These are the earliest texts attributed to the Buddha and many of them (although not all) are simple and practical. Good ones to begin with are the *Dhammapada, Udāna* and *Sutta-Nipāta* – all quite approachable and 'user-friendly', with short sections or chapters that lend themselves to reflective reading. The *Majjhima Nikāya* is a much larger book, with longer chapters, but containing some very interesting stories and teachings. You can read just about every sutta from the Pali canon, often in more than one translation, on the website www.accesstoinsight.com.[9] Once you've read some of those you might want to explore some of the later developments of his teaching, as found in the Mahāyāna and Vajrayana schools.

How do we know the Buddha said it?

I've just written that the texts found in the Pali canon are *attributed* to the Buddha, but we can't be certain that he did in fact say everything that he is quoted as saying in them. In fact there are good reasons to doubt that. The Buddha didn't actually write anything, and the Pali canon was only written some two or three hundred years after he lived, so there were plenty of opportunities for his teachings to be misheard and written down wrongly. But if we can't be sure that the Pali canon contains an accurate record of the Buddha's teaching, how can we rely on them? What authority do they have? Like all Buddhist texts, they stand or fall on their own merits, not because they are supposedly the words of the Buddha. The distinction between extrinsic and intrinsic authority is useful here. Extrinsic authority derives its legitimacy from a source outside of itself:

The Art of Reflection

someone in authority, or perhaps a whole tradition, tells us that a certain text contains the truth, the implication being that we should therefore believe it. Intrinsic authority derives its legitimacy from itself. As Richard Holloway has written in his book *Doubts and Loves*, intrinsic authority 'wins our inner consent by a mysterious process that persuades and draws affirmation from us. We say yes to it, acknowledge that it has a legitimate claim upon us, has caused a powerful act of recognition and mutuality to work within our hearts and minds.'[10] If a poem moves us or sears us with its truth, it doesn't matter who wrote it. We may want to find out who the author was, but only because we would like to read more of their poems, not because we feel the need to legitimize the poem by making sure it was by a 'good' poet. When the Buddha started teaching, people listened to him because he had his own intrinsic authority. After all, who was he? As far as most people were concerned he was just another one of many holy men passing through town. There was no external authority he could call on to legitimize his teaching, even if he had wanted to. People listened to him because they intuited the truth in his words.

If you are not used to reading ancient Buddhist texts you probably won't find them easy at first. There are all sorts of obstacles to overcome, such as the unfamiliar style of writing, the references and allusions to things and people with which you may not be familiar, and sometimes the literary style of the translator. You have to *learn* to read them, and this takes time and patience. You may also need a guide – someone who has studied the texts and can illuminate them for you. If you have a teacher he or she may go through a text with you verbally, or you may read a commentary.[11] Once you have read a few of these commentaries though, and have learned to some extent how to read a text, I would then suggest that you choose a text and reflect on it yourself *before reading the commentary*. Reading commentaries can make us lazy – we can let the commentator do all the work for us. A good sequence is to read a text, reflect on it, then read a commentary on the text, and then reflect on that.

It's also good to 'follow your nose' – simply read what interests you. I have found that if a text, or something in a text, fascinates or attracts me, *there is always something in it for me*. There is some treasure buried there, something in that text that I need to know, that I need to realize, that will help me to grow. It's also worth reading texts that you don't like. Of course we tend to avoid whatever we don't like, but you might try reading it anyway to see what happens. I've always disliked Shantideva's *Bodhicaryāvatāra* because it has intimidated me. His instructions and exhortations are so uncompromising that I have always felt that I am an inferior sort of Buddhist when I read it, unable to meet the required expectations. Perhaps this is why Pierre Hadot says that reading texts is one of the most difficult of spiritual practices – and certainly when we read a Buddhist text we are encountering an Enlightened mind, and this encounter can feel very uncomfortable. However, while on a solitary retreat recently, I recited part of the *Bodhicaryāvatāra*, and found, to my surprise, that I enjoyed it! Perhaps I have changed!

Incidentally, there's an important point to be made here about what we expect from Buddhist texts. If we approach them primarily as 'instruction manuals' we may miss something very important – their beauty and inspiration. Some texts in fact contain no instructions at all. They might, for instance, describe the characteristics of a wise man, but say nothing about how we might ourselves become wise. Or they may simply tell a story. Or they may, in the case of some Mahāyāna sūtras (sūtra is the Sanskrit form of sutta), describe a fantastic universe. If we look for teachings in such texts we'll be disappointed, but only because we're looking for the wrong thing. With texts that give us practical instructions on how to live the spiritual life, we read them so that we can practise their teachings once we put the book down. In the cases of texts that describe the wise, or tell stories, or describe amazing world-systems, reading them *is* the practice. All that we need to do is open ourselves up to them as if they were poetry or story books, and let ourselves be changed by them.

To read in this way, it is better to read aloud. As children we learned to read by vocalizing the words on the page – we spoke them aloud. As we grew older we learned to read silently, perhaps moving our lips in the first months or years of our silent reading, but eventually not even that. This is a very useful skill because it means that we can read in the presence of others who may not want to hear what we are reading. (Even more useful perhaps is the fact that it enables us to read what others may not want us to read!) However, something is lost when we read silently. Literature, especially poetry, is meant to be *heard*. The words and phrases often have a rhythmical and musical quality that is not only beautiful but also adds emotional weight to the meaning. Buddhist texts have traditionally been read (or chanted) aloud, usually in a ritual context, and in my experience such readings allow me to 'understand' a text much more fully than I've been able to when reading silently. I put the word 'understand' in single inverted commas because I don't mean it in a purely intellectual sense. Saying a word or phrase out loud can help in the process of experiencing, even of *becoming*, what that word or phrase expresses. Not all Buddhist texts are beautiful, but even quite ordinary texts benefit from being read aloud, because that makes us read more slowly, and we've already seen how valuable this can be.

Preparing your state of mind to read a text

Before we read a text we may need to prepare ourselves. If we're in a bad mood or feeling discontented we might project our mood onto the text, finding fault and getting irritated with it. One ancient Buddhist text begins with the words:

> Call forth as much as you can of love, of respect, and of
> faith!
> Remove the obstructing defilements and clear away all
> your taints!
> Listen to the perfect wisdom of the gentle Buddhas,
> Taught for the weal of the world, for heroic spirits
> intended.[12]

This is a translation of a Sanskrit text by the eminent Buddhist scholar Edward Conze, and the word that he translates as love – *prema* – also means affection. By now you will probably have got the message that reflection is at least as much about emotion as it is about reason, so the idea that we need to call forth love and affection before reading a Buddhist text should not seem too surprising. As I wrote in Chapter 2 (page 47), positive emotions can give us the inner resources necessary to understand truths that we may experience as threatening, and Buddhist texts can be very challenging. It's also possible that the text is asking us to love the text itself, or at least, more generally, the Dharma. If so, this would be similar to the idea expressed in the word 'philosophy', which means 'the love of wisdom'.

In this verse 'respect' translates *gaurava*, from the term guru, which literally means 'weighty', that is, significant, of great consequence. The text is telling us that we need to take it seriously because it's got important things to tell us about the way things are and how we can become fit to understand the way things are. It is laden with valuable cargo! This is why Buddhist texts are treated with great reverence in traditional Buddhist cultures, where people wrap them in precious cloths and place them on shrines, never putting them on the floor. I'm reminded of Nietzsche's words 'with delicate eyes and fingers'.

For many people faith is incompatible with freedom of thought because it is associated in their minds with closed-mindedness. To have faith is to believe, and to believe is to be intolerant of any ideas or facts that contradict those beliefs. However, we have to be careful not to be misled by words. Faith is an English word, with its own set of connotations, and we shouldn't assume that the original Sanskrit word shares those connotations. The word translated as faith is *prasāda*, which also means clearness, brightness, pellucidity, purity, calmness, tranquillity, absence of excitement, serenity of disposition, good humour, aid, mediation – in fact, it seems to mean all good things![13] Now, if we replace the word faith at the end of that first line with one of the other meanings of *prasāda* – say clarity, or tranquillity, or good humour – we get a very different meaning. Let's try just one of these to see how it reads:

> Call forth as much as you can of love, of respect and of
> good humour!

That makes a big difference, doesn't it? But what has faith to do with good humour – or clarity, or purity, or tranquillity for that matter? How can one word mean so many things? Well, they are all skilful mental states, and according to the *Abhidharma*, the so-called psychology of Buddhism, faith is present in every skilful mental state. We could say it is the common factor in all skilful states. So whenever you are friendly, or compassionate, or mindful, or patient, or reflective, then you also have faith . . . just think about that for a minute! What might it mean? In Buddhism faith is directed towards the Three Jewels, and particularly towards the fundamental teachings of the Buddha; Buddhists have faith in the Three Jewels and they believe that life is impermanent, insubstantial and ultimately unsatisfactory etc. However, unless the authors of the *Abhidharma* thought that only Buddhists were capable of experiencing skilful mental states (unlikely, I think), they seem to be saying that faith is not so much a belief in certain ideas, as a mental state, or attitude. As we've seen, skilful mental states give us the inner resources to see things more truly. They are more 'open' than unskilful states, which tend to be inward-looking and protective of the self. When we're in a skilful state we're more open to the truth of things, regardless of what implications that truth might have on ourselves. Faith, we could perhaps say, is a state in which we are open to the way things really are. We could even say that faith is open-mindedness. Or empathy (see Paul Gilbert's definition above). But now I'm adding to the number of meanings of *prasāda*, as if it didn't have enough already.

Having respect and faith, therefore, doesn't mean that we have to agree with everything in a Buddhist text. In any case it's unlikely that all Buddhist texts were written by fully Enlightened people, even those that claim to be the word of the Buddha, so we need to read them critically as well as with respect and faith. (In Nietzsche's words, we need to read them 'with reservations' as well as 'with doors left open'.) We don't need to treat Buddhist texts as authority figures that have to be believed. A better way of approaching them might be as we would a wise and kind friend; that is, someone who has our best interests at heart, and whose counsel we value, but with whose opinions we may not always agree. If you *do* disagree with something in a text though, don't *just* disagree; ask yourself *why* you disagree. After all, if you disagreed with something your friend said, he or she would ask you that question, wouldn't they? And they'd probably argue their point too. A text is unable to do that, so you need to be scrupulous in your disagreements. Perhaps you could get into dialogue with the text, in a similar way to that described in Chapter 3, when I discussed talking to yourself as a way of reflecting (page 64). In that section I suggested that you take two sides of an argument and argue for both. In this instance, one voice can be 'you' and the other the text. Remember though, for it to be effective you have to argue for both sides as if you really mean it. Don't let yourself off the hook too easily. After all, you could be wrong!

If we can do that, we are maintaining two values that are important in any learning environment: freedom and respect. We need to feel free to disagree, because we can't give our assent to something unless we feel free to withhold it. To think about something we need the freedom to follow wherever reason may take us, otherwise our thinking will be inhibited, fettered. However, we can disagree with respect. This combination of freedom and respect is unusual, I think, in modern (Western) culture. Media debates are often conducted in an atmosphere of personal animosity, distrust, and disrespect, and this makes it easy for us to assume that disagreement always implies lack of respect. On the other hand it can be hard to disagree with someone for whom we feel great respect – 'Who am I to disagree with him?' It can be difficult to hold both values simultaneously, but it is important that we do. Freedom safeguards our personal integrity and respect allows us to be receptive to others' wisdom.

Translations are interpretations

It's a good idea to read more than one translation of a work if you can. A translation is inevitably an interpretation; a translator has their own understanding of Buddhism and they will interpret a text in the light of that understanding. My teacher once said that reading a translation is like looking at the reverse side of a tapestry – the colours and general shapes are all visible but we are unable to see the exact pattern or design on the front. By reading more than one translation you get different interpretations, and this can give you a better idea of what the front of the tapestry might look like. Here are three different translations of the first two verses of the *Dhammapada*:

1. Experiences are preceded by mind, led by mind, and produced by mind. If one speaks or acts with an impure mind, suffering follows even as the cartwheel follows the hoof of the ox (drawing the cart).

2. Experiences are preceded by mind, led by mind, and produced by mind. If one speaks or acts with a pure mind, happiness follows like a shadow that never departs.[14]

1. We are what we think.
   All that we are arises with our thoughts.
   With our thoughts we make the world.
   Speak or act with an impure mind
   And trouble will follow you
   As the wheel follows the ox that draws the cart.

2. We are what we think.
   All that we are arises with our thoughts.
   With our thoughts we make the world.
   Speak or act with a pure mind
   And happiness will follow you
   As your shadow, unshakable.[15]

1. Phenomena are preceded by the heart,
      ruled by the heart,
      made of the heart.
   If you speak or act
   with a corrupted heart,
   then suffering follows you –
   as the wheel of the cart,
      the track of the ox
      that pulls it.

2. Phenomena are preceded by the heart,
        ruled by the heart,
        made of the heart.
    If you speak or act
    with a calm, bright heart,
    then happiness follows you,
    like a shadow
        that never leaves.[16]

Quite different from one another, aren't they? The first translation has mind as the central subject, the second has thought, and the third has heart. Which is correct? Is one closer to the real meaning of the original than another? Unless you know Pali and have the original in front of you there isn't really a way to tell. We are at the mercy of the translators! Most English translations use 'mind', and that is probably the most accurate translation of the Pali word *mano*, although 'thought' is fine too. Thanissaro, the translator of the third version quoted here, uses 'heart'. He knows his Pali, no question, so he hasn't made a mistake; Buddhism considers a mental state to consist in both thoughts and emotions. By using 'heart' he is bringing out the part that emotions play in our suffering and happiness.[17] So you see how different translations can give quite different interpretations of a text.

There is a lot to reflect on in these verses – it's no accident that they come right at the beginning of the *Dhammapada*. Let's remind ourselves of Nietzsche's passage on slow reading: 'read slowly, deeply, looking cautiously before and aft, with reservations, with doors left open, with delicate eyes and fingers'. Try reading them aloud a couple of times, *listening* to the words, feeling their meanings. You could begin by reflecting just on the first clause: *Experiences are preceded by mind*, or *We are what we think*, or *Phenomena are preceded by the heart*. What does that mean? What does 'preceded' mean? (We can be pretty sure the translators chose that word carefully to express the Pali meaning as best they could, so we may as well be as careful – look it up in a dictionary.) Is it true that my experiences are preceded by my mind/heart? *Am I what I think?* Is it my experience? What *is* my experience? Do I

The Art of Reflection

know? – that is, have I been mindful enough to notice? If it *is* true, what are the implications for me, for other people, for the world? If I believe it, or know it to be true from my own experience, do I act as if that were the case? Do I *live* that belief or knowledge? If I don't, why not?

So you see, you could spend a lot of time reflecting on these verses. Sangharakshita once said that for every hour of reading we should spend a hundred hours reflecting! (Don't take that too literally – he was just making a point!) You could make use of some of the methods that I described in Chapter 4, such as having a conversation with yourself, writing, or going for a walk. To do the latter you'll need to memorize the verses, which would be a very good thing to do anyway. As I pointed out in the Introduction, the earliest Buddhists didn't have texts, so they memorized one or more of the Buddha's teachings and reflected on them.

The second halves of the verses are similes, so our reflections will proceed a little differently, less analytically, less intellectually, more emotionally, more sensitively, *feeling* our way into the meaning. Thanissaro makes a lovely point in his notes on this verse: 'The images in these verses are carefully chosen. The cart, representing suffering, is a burden on the ox pulling it, and the weight of its wheels obliterates the ox's track. The shadow, representing happiness, is no weight on the body at all.' We can reflect on that. Of course, in the West the metaphor of the shadow is often a negative one, perhaps because of Jung's archetypes, where the shadow represents those aspects of ourselves that exclude information from consciousness about our true motivations, and is 'dark, shadowy, unknown and potentially troubling.'[18] However, if we remember that the Buddha lived in India – a very hot place – we can see how the shadow might symbolize something very pleasant and welcome – cool. We could then go on to think about the Buddha sitting under the shade of the Bodhi Tree . . . and so on. You could write an essay or give a talk on just these two verses!

Reading our own meanings into a text

All translations are interpretations, and if the translator has some understanding of Buddhism, you won't be misled too far. What do you make of this?

> Believe nothing, no matter where you read it or who has said it, not even if I have said it, unless it agrees with your own reason and your own common sense.
>
> The Buddha

This is something that I found on the internet, and which I've also seen on a postcard. Did the Buddha *really* say that? I would be surprised if he did, as it is not consistent with many other things he said. It's interesting that neither the internet quote nor the postcard gives a reference as to where we might find it. Is it perhaps a corrupted version of what the Buddha says in the *Kalāma Sutta*?

> Do not go upon what has been acquired by repeated hearing; nor upon tradition; nor upon rumour; nor upon what is in a scripture; nor upon surmise; nor upon an axiom; nor upon specious reasoning; nor upon a bias toward a notion that has been pondered over; nor upon another's seeming ability; nor upon the consideration, 'The monk is our teacher'. Kalamas, when you yourselves know: 'These things are bad; these things are blamable; these things are censured by the wise; undertaken and observed, these things lead to harm and ill,' abandon them.[19]

If the first of the two quotes above *is* a corrupted translation of this passage from the *Kalāma Sutta*, it is only an extreme version of what we all tend to do – read our own meanings and values into a text. This is perhaps another reason why Hadot says that reading texts is one of the hardest of spiritual exercises – because it is *so* hard to read what the text actually says. One of the things that prevents us from being able to read what's on the page is our cultural conditioning and prejudices, that is, the ways of seeing the world and the values that we've imbibed from our parents, teachers, friends, the media etc. These are usually invisible to us, like spectacles, so that we don't even realize we're reading a text through them. When they are invisible to us they are called *assumptions* because we assume that the way we see things is the way things are. In the example above, it would seem that the translator was trying to read into the text a form of rationalism: 'Believe nothing!'

As our assumptions are unconscious you might think there is nothing we can do about them, but actually there is something we can do – try to read what is actually on the page! This is surprisingly difficult to do, as I know from my experience of writing about and speaking about texts. I'll have written a paragraph or two about a certain passage and then when I re-read the same passage later I realize I'd previously misread it. Goethe was aware of this difficulty when he wrote: 'Ordinary people don't know how much time and effort it takes to learn how to read. I've spent eighty years at it, and I still can't say that I've reached my goal.'[20]

It's surprising how often readers (and writers) miss a small but important phrase in the *Kalāma Sutta* passage. They see 'when you yourselves know: "These things are bad; these things are blamable"', but they miss "These things are censured by the wise". This allows them to interpret the Buddha as saying that the Kalamas should go by their own direct experience, which is only half of what the text is saying. What the Buddha said was that they should go by their own experience *and* by what the wise say. Why do you think people tend to miss that little phrase (which, by the way, is repeated a number of times in the sutta)? I suspect it's because they *want* the Buddha to be saying that they should only go by their own experience. I suspect that they *don't* want the Buddha to say that we should also listen to those who are wise, and so they don't notice it. What cultural conditioning, what assumptions do you think these readers and writers are reading the text through? And what assumptions do you think you bring to your reading?

Living with a text

Buddhist literature, as I've already said, is vast, and we could spend our whole lives reading it all. While that might be a very good thing to do, it's also valuable to spend some time on a few texts, or even just one, so that you can gain a depth of understanding. It's good to live with one text for a while, for many months, or even years. In this way you develop a relationship – a friendship – with the text. You can in fact come to love a text. A while ago I decided to give a series of talks on the fourth and fifth chapters of the *Sutta Nipāta*, considered by many scholars to be the oldest parts of the Pali canon.[21] Ten years previously I had given a talk on them and had felt that there was much more in these texts to be explored. I took them on a solitary retreat and thought about them for an hour or two each day. They are simple texts, not intellectually demanding, and after a few days I began to feel a little worried: 'There is not much in these texts after all, and I shall have nothing to say in my series of talks.' However, by just living with these texts for a few weeks, returning to them every day, slowly they revealed themselves to me.

A text *slowly* reveals itself because you can only understand it to the extent of your spiritual development. You may have had the experience of re-reading a book or an article that you had previously read a few years ago, and being astonished to read something that you can't remember at all from your previous reading. This may be because you have simply forgotten that passage, but this only prompts another question – why did you so utterly forget it? Probably because it wasn't relevant to you at the time, so you simply didn't notice it. My teacher Sangharakshita once said, with regard to a Buddhist text, that 'you are drawn to a teaching when you are ready for it. It is as though the teaching is moving towards you at the same time that you are moving towards it.'[22]

I have already quoted Pierre Hadot saying 'let the texts speak to us', I have just written about texts 'revealing themselves', and now I've quoted Sangharakshita talking about teachings 'moving towards' us. All these phrases suggest a relationship, with the text playing an active role. This may seem strange, in that a text is just a piece of paper (or perhaps a computer screen) with words on it. A text is inert, without consciousness, so how can *it* relate to *us*? Assuming that a text is a teaching given by an Enlightened or partially Enlightened being, it will be multi-layered, by which I mean that it will be possible to understand the teaching at different levels. Understanding the teaching at a lower level will not exhaust the meaning. There will be higher or deeper understandings to be gained, and in this sense the text has more to say than that which we are able to hear, or understand, at present. So in a sense the text is *waiting* for us to understand the meaning more fully or deeply and speaks to us, reveals itself, or moves towards us when we are ready.

Wisdom has depths that we do not – cannot – access immediately, and the only way to access these depths is to come into relationship with the text, pondering it, revisiting it from time to time, and allowing ourselves to change so that we can access the deeper meanings. Thus to reflect on a text is not to gain more information about it – although that may also happen – but to become a different person.

> There are some truths whose meaning will never be exhausted by the generations of man. It is not that they are difficult; on the contrary they are often extremely simple. Often, they even appear to be banal. Yet for their meaning to be understood, these truths must be lived, and constantly re-experienced. Each generation must take up, from scratch, the task of learning to read and re-read these 'old truths'.[23]
>
> Pierre Hadot

Chapter Five

·····························

Imagining the Buddha

Whatever you frequently think and ponder upon,
that will become the inclination of your mind.[1]

The Buddha

Do you know anyone who is wise? If so, take a few moments to think about them. What are they like? What is it about them that makes you think they are wise? In what ways are they wise? Of course it's unlikely that you'll know someone who is *completely* wise in every respect. Probably they are wise in some ways, or at some times, and not so wise in other ways, or at other times. So think about them at their best, when they *are* being wise. If you don't know anyone whom you consider to be wise, think about what a wise person *may be* like. Use your imagination. You should be able to do this because, if you don't know anyone who is wise, you must then have an idea of what a wise person must be like, i.e. not like anyone you know! For instance, if you consider someone to be unwise because they are very touchy and don't take criticism at all well, then you must think that a wise person is someone who listens to criticism without feeling upset. Or if you consider someone to be unwise who likes to win arguments, you must think that a wise person is not concerned with winning arguments, but is more concerned with discovering the truth. Another thing you could do is think about a fictional character from a story – say a novel or a film.

Most of us, I think, have some idea of what a wise person is like, or would be like, if we were to meet one. In a study carried

·····························

out in 1980, two psychologists asked a number of participants what they thought were the main characteristics of wise people. Once they had gathered everyone's responses, they found that the characteristics people chose naturally clustered around three areas: affective (i.e. emotional), reflective and cognitive. The affective qualities people mentioned were peaceful, empathetic, understanding, and gentle; the reflective characteristics were introspective and intuitive; and the cognitive were pragmatic, observant, and intelligent.[2]

Now, thinking about this wise person whom *you* know, or an imaginary one, do you recognize any qualities that they possess in the above list? Are there other qualities that you think should be added to the list? What are they? You could make your own list. Once you have thought about this for a while, spend some time reflecting on these qualities. Don't just *think* about them, try to *feel* your way into them. Try to understand what it might be like to have these wise qualities. What might it be like to be someone who is, say, peaceful, empathetic, understanding, gentle, introspective, intuitive, observant, and intelligent?

Reflecting on the qualities of the wise was apparently taught and practised in the ancient Greek and Roman schools of philosophy. According to Pierre Hadot:

> In the teaching of ancient philosophy, a major role was played by the discourse which consisted in describing the sage. It was less important to trace the features of concrete particularly noteworthy philosophers or sages . . . than to define the sage's ideal behaviour, and ask: 'What would the sage do in such-and-such circumstances?'[3]

Why? Well, in a way there is no such thing as wisdom; that is, wisdom doesn't exist as an abstract quality, somewhere out there in the universe, that we have to try to get hold of. There are only wise people. So if we want to see what wisdom is like, we need to look at people who are wise, people who *embody* wisdom.

Reflecting on the qualities of the wise – that is, the way wisdom is expressed in wise individuals – can encourage and inspire us to emulate them. If other people can become wise, so can we. Also, by reflecting on the qualities of the wise we tend to become a little wiser ourselves. To see how this might work, let's take the first of the qualities mentioned in the study I quoted above. Wise individuals, people thought, were peaceful. Peacefulness, then, seems to be an expression of wisdom. Now, we can become peaceful by being wise, *or we can become wise by being peaceful*. That is, a peaceful state of mind tends to make us a little wiser, or at least a little more inclined to be wise. Isn't it true that when we are agitated, upset, anxious or stressed out, we are liable to make unwise decisions, decisions that we might regret later? Conversely, when we're in a very calm state, we tend to make wiser decisions. By trying to put ourselves into the state of mind of a wise person, we begin to see the world as a wise person sees it.

We can go a little further than this. A wise person will *behave* differently from the way an unwise person behaves. For instance, if those people interviewed by the two psychologists in 1980 were right, wise people are understanding and gentle, and these qualities will be expressed in their behaviour: they will *be* understanding and gentle in their interactions with other people. (Remember that 'understanding' was put in the affective – i.e. emotional – category, so it means 'tolerant and sympathetic towards other people' rather than understanding in the more cognitive sense.) If we *behave* wisely – that is, *as if* we were already wise – that behaviour tends to make us wiser. This is one of the reasons Buddhists practise ethics; when we're ethical we're behaving as if we were already wise. How is this? A wise person will be spontaneously understanding and gentle; it won't be an effort for them, it will be a natural expression of the way they see the world and other people. To the extent that we're unwise, we won't always feel like being understanding or gentle, but if we make an effort to *be* understanding and gentle anyway, then we're practising ethics – we're behaving *as if* we were wise. And this behaviour will tend to make us a little wiser.

In his book *The Compassionate Mind* Paul Gilbert offers a number of exercises to help us develop compassion. One of these exercises is to get into the role of a wise, compassionate person, as if you're an actor. To do it successfully, he says, you have to get in touch with what it is to *be that person*:

> Imagine that you are a deeply compassionate and wise person. Think of the ideal qualities that you would like to have . . . These might include deep kindness, warmth, gentleness, being difficult to provoke, a sense of having 'been there' and gaining wisdom as a result. It doesn't matter if you actually have these qualities or not, because you're focussing on imagining and thinking about what it would be like to have them, what they are and your desire to develop them.[4]

Characteristics of a Buddha

Reflecting on the qualities of the wise is also practised within the Buddhist tradition. Specifically, we are recommended to reflect on the qualities of an Enlightened person – that is, someone who is completely wise. This is called the practice of *Buddhānussati*. *Anussati* means recollection, remembrance, and by extension, calling to mind, keeping in mind, bearing in mind. It is one of a set of meditation practices – actually a number of sets – called the *anussatis*. There is a set of three, which lists the qualities of the Buddha, Dharma, and Sangha. There is also a set of six, consisting of the three that I've just mentioned plus ethics, generosity, and the *devas* (the mythological gods of Indian tradition). Finally, there is a list of ten: the six already mentioned plus the breath, death, the body, and calmness. In the earliest (Pali) literature no one *anussati* seems to be valued above the others, but in the later, Mahāyāna literature, only the first three (Buddha, Dharma, and Sangha) are considered to be important, and *Buddhānussati* the most important of these.

There is a text in the Pali canon that is traditionally recommended for this reflection called the *Buddhavandana*, or

Homage to the Buddha:

> Indeed, the Blessed One is worthy & rightly self-awakened, consummate in knowledge & conduct, well-gone, knower of the cosmos, unexcelled trainer of those who can be tamed, teacher of devas and human beings, awakened, blessed.[5]

For many people this short text will appear quite opaque, and they will need the help of either someone who knows the text or a written commentary that explains the significance of each of the qualities enumerated. It also assumes some prior knowledge of and faith in the Buddha, and for this reason I would recommend first reading a few other texts that describe the Buddha more fully, such as the *Purabheda Sutta*, from a book called the *Sutta-Nipāta*. In this text someone asks the Buddha what a 'man of calm' is like – how they see things and how they behave. Most scholars agree that the *Purabheda Sutta* is among the oldest texts in the Pali canon, and in these very old texts calmness is one of the main ways the Buddha and others refer to the goal of the Buddhist life – what would later be called *Bodhi* or Nirvana: Enlightenment or awakening. A 'man of calm', therefore, is someone who is wise. (Incidentally, here we return to a topic we touched on in the Introduction, when I discussed D. H. Lawrence's use of *man* and *his* in his poem 'Thought'. Like Lawrence, Pali texts invariably use the masculine pronoun, as do most other traditional Buddhist texts in other languages. If you are sensitive to this use of language, and particularly if you are female and feel excluded by it, then reading traditional texts could be problematic for you. It is clear from the Buddha's teachings in other parts of the Pali canon that he thought that women could become wise, and many of his female disciples did in fact gain Enlightenment. So if you *are* sensitive to this, I think it's valid to amend the phrase 'man of calm' to 'a woman of calm' or, to be really inclusive, to the non-gender specific 'someone who is calm'. You would then also need to replace 'he' and 'his' in the quotation below to 'she' and 'her' or to 'they'. If you decide to be non-gender-specific you'll have to change some of the grammar accordingly; instead of 'He has no anger', for instance, you'll need to write 'They have no anger'.)

The Buddha replies with a list of characteristics, most of which I have reproduced below. I haven't included his answer in full, partly because there is some repetition, but also because sometimes the meaning of a passage is a little obscure. It wouldn't be appropriate to go into all the different possible interpretations of these obscure passages here because my aim is to write a practical book on reflection rather than a work of philology. Therefore I've used a translation by Saddhatissa, who has 'tidied up' some passages to make it more easily readable. While it may not be technically accurate in every verse, it's close enough for us to get a pretty good idea of what a wise person is like.

> He has no anger, no fear and no pride. Nothing disturbs his composure and nothing gives him cause for regret. He is the wise man who is restrained in speech.

> He does not conceal anything and there is nothing he holds on to. Without acquisitiveness or envy, he remains unobtrusive; he has no disdain or insult for anyone.

> He is not a man who is full of himself, or a man who is addicted to pleasure; he is a man who is gentle and alert, with no blind faith; he shows no aversion [to anything].

> He is not a person who works because he wants something; if he gets nothing at all he remains unperturbed. There is no craving to build up the passion to taste new pleasures.

> His mindfulness holds him poised in a constant even-mindedness where arrogance is impossible; he makes no comparisons with the rest of the world as 'superior', 'inferior' or 'equal'.

> Because he understands the Way Things Are, he is free from dependency and there is nothing he relies on. For him there is no more craving to exist or not to exist.

This is what I call a man who is calmed. It is a man who does not seek after pleasure, who has nothing to tie him down, who has gone beyond the pull of attachment.

It is a man without sons, a man without wealth . . . – a man with nothing in him that he grasps at as his and nothing in him that he rejects as not his.

He is a man who receives false criticisms from other people . . . but who remains undisturbed and unmoved by their words.[6]

So this is what the Buddha said a wise person was like, and one of the interesting things about it is that there is only one reference to understanding in the more cognitive sense: 'he understands the Way Things Are'. The rest of the verses describe how he (or she) feels: 'he has no anger, no fear and no pride' or does: 'he remains unobtrusive . . . does not seek after pleasure'. Wisdom is often thought of in terms of *knowing* or *understanding*, but it is at least as much about *being* a certain kind of way. As I have already mentioned, there are a few Pali texts that describe the qualities of an Enlightened person, but none of them specifically mention one very important quality of wisdom: kindness or compassion. It is often *implied* – for instance, in the *Purabheda Sutta,* in qualities such as gentleness and having 'no disdain or insult for anyone' – but not specifically mentioned. However, there is one really striking passage in a text that describes the death of the Buddha. Just a few moments before the Buddha dies, his closest friend, Ananda, leans against a doorpost and weeps, saying 'The Teacher is passing away, he who was so kind to me.' As I said, Ananda was the Buddha's closest friend and he lived with him for many years. He heard countless teachings by him, and yet the thing that he said of him as he was dying was that he was kind. Kindness is a form of wisdom. I'll say more about this at the end of this chapter.

One way of practising *Buddhānussati* is to take a text like the *Purabheda Sutta* and reflect on each of the qualities mentioned, one by one. For instance, we could reflect on the line 'he makes no comparisons with the rest of the world as "superior", "inferior"

The Art of Reflection

or "equal"'. Most of us compare ourselves with others in various ways: 'he is better-looking than I am', 'she earns more than I do', 'he is not as intelligent as me', 'she is less popular than I am', 'he is about as grey as I am', 'her car must have cost about the same as mine'. A wise person, apparently, doesn't do that. They don't even think of themselves as being equal to others. So, why not? What is unwise about comparing oneself with others? How much do I do it? What effect does it have on me? How does it affect my relationships with the people I'm comparing myself with? What would it be like not to compare myself with anyone?

While we're on the topic of comparing, one thing to beware of when reflecting on the qualities of the wise is the tendency to compare ourselves unfavourably with them. Say you begin to reflect on the qualities of a wise person that you know. This is how it could go: 'He is so wise, so great; he's kind and always has a good word for everyone; he never snaps at people – not like me, irritable and bad-tempered. Only yesterday I was grumpy with everyone. How do I expect to become wise like him?' Before you know it you're beating yourself up for not being like that wise person, and that's not the purpose of the exercise! In a Mahāyāna text called the *Vimalakīrti-nirdeśa* (the *Teaching of Vimalakīrti*), the layman/Bodhisattva Vimalakīrti sings the praises of Bodhisattvas, and one verse goes like this:

> Though they worship Buddhas by the millions,
> With every conceivable offering,
> They never dwell upon the least difference
> Between the Buddhas and themselves.

This is very interesting. 'Looking up to' is not the same as 'comparing with'. When reflecting on the qualities of the wise we don't need to even consider whether we have that quality or not, and if we do, to what degree. We don't need to think about ourselves at all in fact. The important thing is to focus on the quality, not on ourselves. It could be that we haven't developed that particular quality very much at all, or we may have already developed it to quite a high degree. From the point of view of reflecting on the quality it doesn't matter: we can always develop it more than we have already!

Moving from reflection to contemplation

There is another way, however, of practising *Buddhānussati*, and with this we encounter a quite different kind of reflection to the one we've been mainly considering in this book so far. Up until now we have been exploring reflection in its more analytical, discursive, thinking aspect, but there is another kind. In this sort of reflection we don't have many thoughts, we don't have lots of words in our heads, we don't talk to ourselves, we don't follow a line of argument. It is more meditative, more silent, more still, more serene. (I did touch on this very briefly in Chapter 3, page 73 but now we're going to explore it more fully.) I'm going to call it contemplation to distinguish it from the more discursive kind of reflection I've been describing up until now. To contemplate is 'to look at with continued attention, gaze upon, observe'. It comes from the Latin *contemplare*, which, my old *Oxford Universal Dictionary* tells me, is 'an open place for observation marked out by the augur', i.e. a soothsayer, diviner, or prophet.[7] I like this idea of an open space – when we contemplate we metaphorically open up a space in our minds, a space free from words and thoughts, and we try to dwell in that space so that we can simply 'gaze upon, observe', free from commentary. In the words of D. H. Lawrence's poem, contemplation, we could say, is 'looking onto the face of life and reading what can be read'.

To practise *Buddhānussati* as a contemplation, we 'look at with continued attention' each of the Buddha's qualities, but without thinking about them. This works well if you have first reflected on the quality in a more analytical way. Now, understanding that quality better, appreciating its value and perhaps developing an aspiration to realize it in ourselves, we can let go of all our thinking *about* the quality, and enter into a quieter, less busy contemplation *of* it. We don't need to continue to rehearse the arguments in its favour or deal with all possible objections or think about its implications; now we just look at it. In doing that we are trying to *intuit* that quality. Intuition comes from the Latin *intueri*, which means 'to look inside', and when we contemplate we're not just looking *at*, or *onto*, but also *into*. So when we contemplate one of the Buddha's qualities we try to *feel* our way inside it, to inhabit

The Art of Reflection

it, and look out at the world from the perspective of that quality. We try to *become* the quality, that is, to realize it in ourselves.

Have a go yourself. Take a quality and reflect on it, think about it, ask questions of it, try to imagine what it would be like to have that quality; and then stop thinking. Stop talking! Just bear it in mind. Feel its presence. Be with it for a while, in the way that you might be with a friend after having talked for hours, now just enjoying their presence in companionable silence. Once we have practised for some time in this way, reflecting and contemplating on each of the qualities in turn, there will come a point when all we really need do is call to mind the word 'Buddha': all of the qualities we have reflected on will be encapsulated in that one word. It's like any name. When you are first introduced to someone, their name is just a label, more or less. As you get to know them, however, their name signifies more and more, so that when you say or think their name, it *means* more because it holds everything that you know about them.

Just as the name 'Buddha' can hold all of the Buddha's qualities, so can a picture, and another way of practising *Buddhānussati* is to visualize him. To do this, choose a picture or a statue of a Buddha that you like, and look at it for some time. Whenever your mind wanders, bring it back to the contemplation of the image. Then close your eyes and try to see the image in your mind's eye. If any thoughts arise, try to let them go. It can be a simple, 'human' image – a picture of the Buddha as he might have appeared in India 2,500 years ago – or you might prefer something more archetypal: a Buddha with golden skin, or perhaps a different colour – red, blue, green or white – with rays of light emanating from his body. There are plenty of instances of this kind of contemplation in Mahāyāna sūtras, such as the *Sutra of Golden Light* and the *Contemplation of Amitayus Sutra*. By visualizing the Buddha as, say, the colour of gold, his fine features expressing serene joy, with golden light emanating from him in all directions, lighting up the whole universe, we are *imaginatively* contemplating the Buddha's qualities. That is, rather than reflecting or contemplating on the quality of, for instance, gentleness, we *see* that quality expressed in his smile or in the gesture of his fingers.

Contemplating with the whole of our being

As I stated above, the *Buddhānussati* practice was considered the most important of the *anussatis* in the literature of the Mahāyāna. In fact it was probably the basis of the later visualization practices found in many Chinese and Tibetan Buddhist traditions. You may have noticed that in the verse I quoted from the *Vimalakīrti-nirdeśa* above, it refers to *Buddhas* in the plural. In the early (Pali) Buddhist texts there was only one Buddha – the man who lived in India, gained Enlightenment and then taught the Dharma. However, in Mahāyāna Buddhism the idea developed of many Buddhas, existing in different areas of the universe, all with their own Buddha-fields (world-systems, or perhaps galaxies). Just as the name and image of the Buddha encapsulates all of his qualities, so a Buddha-field symbolizes his influence, therefore the Dharma, and the beings living in that land symbolize the (ideal) Sangha. The most well-known of these is the Buddha Amitābha and his Buddha-field Sukhāvatī (the Land of Bliss), which form the doctrinal and mythical basis of the Chinese and Japanese Pure Land traditions. In the (Shorter) *Sukhāvatīvyūha Sutra*, the Buddha describes this land to Śāripūtra, and at one point he says this:

> Furthermore, Śariputra, when the rows of palm trees
> and nets of tinkling bells in that Buddhafield sway in the
> wind, a sweet and enrapturing sound issues from them.
> This concert of sounds is, Śariputra, like a set of heavenly
> cymbals, with a hundred thousand million playing parts
> – when these cymbals are played by expert musicians,
> a sweet and enrapturing sound issues from them. In
> exactly the same way, a sweet and enrapturing sound
> proceeds from those rows of palm trees and those nets of
> tinkling bells when they sway in the wind. When human
> beings in that world hear this sound, they remember
> the Buddha and feel his presence in their whole body,
> they remember the Dharma and feel its presence in their
> whole body, and they remember the Sangha and feel its
> presence in their whole body.[8]

The Art of Reflection

You may be thinking that we are now a very long way from the kind of reflection that we have been so far exploring in this book. You may even think that we have now entered a fantasy world, a million miles away from the reasoned, conceptual kind of reflection with which we started. However, we are still, in fact, very much concerned with reflection. We are just using a different language – the language of symbols, which as the theologian Paul Tillych pointed out, is the language of faith. In this excerpt the beings in Sukhāvatī contemplate the Buddha, Dharma, and Sangha – the first set of three *anussatis*. As I have said, the beings of that land symbolize the ideal Sangha, so we are being shown the ideal way to practise the *anussatis*. The 'sweet and enrapturing sounds' coming from the palm trees, the jewelled nets, and the heavenly cymbals played by the musicians, symbolize the extremely positive mental states experienced in the *dhyānas*. The Buddha then goes on to say that 'they remember the Buddha and feel his presence in their whole body.' We've seen that to contemplate is 'to look at with continued attention, gaze upon, observe', but 'looking' is really a metaphor. We may not be literally looking at something; we may be listening or bearing something in mind. 'Looking' means attending, with any one or more of our senses. The text is telling us that when we practise *Buddhānussati* we should try to feel the presence of the Buddha in our whole body. We could take this literally, although I suspect that 'body' here means our whole being, including our mind and heart. Ideally, contemplation includes all of our senses, all of our faculties. The sūtras that describe Sukhāvatī invite the reader to imagine the Buddha, the land and the inhabitants; not just to visualize them, but to imaginatively hear, smell and feel them too.

To contemplate is to imagine, and we only really imagine when the whole of our being is involved. Of course we can't always achieve that quality of imagination. In my own case, for instance, for much of the time I'm not fully present when I'm trying to contemplate the Buddha: other thoughts and ideas continue to arise. Part of me is contemplating the Buddha and part of me is doing something else. I'm multi-tasking! Every so often though, something happens: there is a sort of shift in my being, and it feels like I am *entering into* the contemplation with my whole being, including my body. It's a little like the difference between driving through some countryside in a car, looking out at the countryside from inside the car; and then stopping, getting out of the car and walking in the countryside. Now you are *in* it rather than looking *at* it: now you can feel the ground underneath your feet; feel the breeze on your skin; smell the fresh air, perhaps scented by pine trees or flowers or the sea; now you can hear the wind, the birdsong etc. You have entered into the countryside and it's all around you. You are now part of it, rather than being a spectator. Unlike getting out of the car though, I can't consciously decide to enter into contemplation. On those rare (blessed!) occasions when I do manage to enter into the contemplation with my whole being, *something happens*, and this does not seem to be within my conscious control. All I can do is contemplate the Buddha to the best of my ability and hope for the best! D. H. Lawrence says in his poem that 'thought is man in his wholeness, wholly attending.' This is a very exalted conception of thought, and is probably quite rare. We usually attend with as much of ourselves as we can muster. To *wholly* attend, in our *wholeness*, is a very different experience. When we are wholly attending, we are imagining.

Of course I am using the word 'imagination' in a very special way here. Imagination has a whole host of meanings: we can imagine walking down a road or entering a room; we can imagine having a different job, having a conversation with someone, or having sex with them; we can imagine being rich and famous, or saving someone's life and becoming a hero; or we can imagine this world being run very differently, as John Lennon did in his famous song. My teacher, Sangharakshita, uses the term 'imaginal faculty' to denote the kind of imagination I've been trying to describe, and to distinguish it from other meanings of the word, such as fancy, whim or fantasy. In a paper called *Journey to Il Convento*, he writes:

> The imaginal faculty is, in reality, the man himself,
> because when one truly perceives an image one
> perceives it with the whole of oneself, or with one's
> whole being. When one truly perceives an image,

The Art of Reflection

therefore, one is transported to the world to which that image belongs and becomes, if only for the time being, an inhabitant of that world. In other words, truly to perceive an image means to become an image, so that when one speaks of the imagination, or the imaginal faculty, what one is really speaking of is image perceiving image. That is to say, in perceiving an image what one really perceives is, in a sense, oneself.[9]

Exactly what the second half of that quotation means – 'image perceiving image' – is difficult to say. The imagination can't be pinned down by the language of reason. The meanings perceived by the imagination are less defined, more suggestive and intuitive than the meanings perceived by reason, and they communicate things that reason by itself is unable to communicate. So rather than trying to understand the meaning of the above quotation in rational terms, it would be better if we tried to intuit the meaning.

Faith and the imagination

Anyway, what does it mean to understand something? We all know that it's possible to understand something with our intellect, but fail to act on that knowledge: we might, for instance, know that eating a lot of rich food is bad for us, but continue to eat it. In that case, do we *really* understand that rich food is bad for us? Presumably not, even though we know all the facts and statistics. Perhaps we could say that we know it and don't know it at the same time. Or we could say that a part of us knows it and a part of us doesn't. We are divided, and the stronger part of ourselves wins. For most of us, our knowledge and understanding is partial in this kind of way: we want to be kind, but find ourselves being snappy at times; we want to be reasonable, but sometimes we behave very irrationally. What we need to do is make our knowledge whole, that is, we need to understand with the whole of our being, and we can only really do that when we *imagine*, in the sense that I've described it here. We only really, wholly, understand how things are when we perceive the world imaginatively.

There is a beautiful description of this state in the novel *Brick Lane* by Monica Ali. The heroine of the story, Nazneen, is one day sitting on the floor of her living room, watching ice skating on the TV, and: 'While she sat, she was no longer a collection of the hopes, random thoughts, petty anxieties and selfish wants that made her, but was whole and pure. The old Nazneen was sublimated and the new Nazneen was filled with white light, glory.'[10] When the whole of oneself is present, something new comes into play: we become more than the sum of our parts. It is only from that state of wholeness, in which we become *more than we are*, that we can really, wholly, understand something. Nazneen experienced wholeness, and with this, purity, white light and glory. We could say the Imagination. We could also say *prasāda*, which, as we saw in Chapter 4, means faith, clearness, brightness, pellucidity, purity, calmness, tranquillity, absence of excitement, serenity of disposition, good humour. At its highest level, faith *is* the imagination.

In his book *Buddhist Meditation* Vajiraṭāna Mahāthera writes of some of the benefits of practising *Buddhānussati*:

> In the mind of him who meditates on the Recollection of the Buddha, the thoughts arise repeatedly with reference to the Buddha's virtue. With the consequent exaltation of mind, full of joy and gladness, he becomes increasingly strengthened in faith and devotion. He realizes the Buddha in his inner being and constantly feels that he is in the presence of the Buddha . . . There arises within him a feeling of a certain intimacy with the Buddha; for he keeps his mind constantly identified with the virtues of the Buddha, so that his body is, as it were, inhabited by a mind continually recollecting this virtue and thus it becomes worthy of adoration, as if it were a shrine.[11]

There is a beautiful passage at the end of the *Sutta-Nipāta*, one of the earliest texts of the Pali canon, in which an old man, Piṇgiya, seems to describe this experience. He is telling his (former?) teacher, a Brahmin, how, since his first meeting with the Buddha, he has not parted from him:

I see him with my mind as if with my eye, being vigilant
day and night, brahman, I pass the night revering him.
For that very reason I think there is no staying away
from him.

My faith and rapture, mind and mindfulness do not stay
away from the teaching of Gotama. In whatever direction
the one of great wisdom goes, in that very direction I
bow down.

I am old and of feeble strength. For that very reason
my body does not go there. I go constantly on a mental
journey, for my mind, brahman, is joined to him.[12]

The Buddha then tells Piṅgiya that, just as others have become
Enlightened through faith, so will he. Wisdom can be realized
through faith. What does this mean? On a certain level it means
that we need to *believe* in the Buddha's teachings: if we don't
believe in their truth, then we won't take them seriously and
practise them. However, belief is only another kind of partial
knowledge. We might believe, for instance, what the Buddha said
about ethics, but we might still behave unethically sometimes. It is
obvious that what Piṅgiya is talking about is not belief in this sense.
He hasn't spoken about his *belief* in the teachings of the Buddha,
he has described his direct experience of *seeing* the Buddha – of
imagining him. Piṅgiya is talking about the imagination, and when
the Buddha tells him that he will gain Enlightenment through
faith, he is saying that he will realize the truth of things through
the imagination. Let's explore this in a little more detail.

The *Milinda-pañha* (the *Questions of King Milinda*) is an
imaginative record of a series of conversations between the
Bactrian Greek King Milinda, who ruled in the Punjab, and the
Indian monk Nāgasena. At a certain point in the text the king
asks Nāgasena what is the characteristic mark of faith, and
Nāgasena replies that there are in fact two characteristic marks:
'tranquillization' and 'aspiration' (or 'leaping forward'). The king
asks him to explain how tranquillization is a mark of faith, and
Nāgasena replies:

As faith, O king, springs up in the heart it breaks through
the five hindrances, and the heart, free from these
hindrances, becomes clear, pure, and serene.[13]

The king then asks Nāgasena to give a simile, which he does.
A king and his army are marching through the land when they
come to a river. They cross the river, causing the water to become
'foul, turbid, and muddy'. The king then becomes thirsty and
asks his men to bring him some water from the river to drink.
Luckily they have brought with them the 'water-purifying gem',
which, when placed in water, immediately causes it to become
'clear, pure, and serene'. In this simile the water is the mind and
the water-purifying gem is, of course, faith. (Incidentally, the Pali
word translated as faith here is *pasāda*, which is the Pali form of
the Sanskrit *prasāda*.)

The five hindrances are: 1) desire for sense experience; 2)
ill-will; 3) restlessness and anxiety; 4) laziness and drowsiness;
and 5) doubt and indecision. They are called hindrances because
they hinder us from experiencing *dhyāna*. Nāgasena tells the King
that when the heart is free of these five hindrances it naturally
enters into the *dhyānas*. Traditionally there are six '*dhyāna* factors'
(*dhyānanga*) or skilful mental states that are present in *dhyāna*.
These are one-pointedness (*ekagatta*), initial thought (*vitakka*),
sustained thought (*vicāra*), rapture (*pīti*), bliss (*sukha*) and
equanimity (*upekṣā*) – the last one emerging only in the fourth
dhyāna. However, *dhyāna* doesn't *only* consist of these factors;
there are other positive qualities present in *dhyāna*. Remember
that, according to the *Abhidharma*, faith is present in every skilful
mental state, which means it must be present in *dhyāna*. We can
think of the four *dhyānas* as increasing and deepening levels of
faith – or states of deepening imagination.

Next, the king asks Nāgasena to tell him about the second
mark of faith – aspiration. He replies that, on seeing that the minds
of others are freed, one leaps forward to the fruit of Stream Entry,
or Once-returning, Non-returning, or Arahantship. (Without
getting into technical doctrinal detail, let's just say that these
are all stages of wisdom, the last one being Enlightenment.) The

king once again asks for a simile, which Nāgasena gives. A heavy rain has caused a river to flood and a great crowd of people are standing on this shore, wanting to cross to the other side, but 'being ignorant of the real breadth or depth of the water . . . stand fearful and hesitating on the brink'.[14] Then a strong man comes along and leaps right across, and seeing this, the great crowd of people standing on this shore are inspired to follow him. You may remember that in the introduction I wrote that crossing the river is one of the most well-known Buddhist similes: this side of the river represents ignorance, while the further shore is Enlightenment. There I mentioned two ways of crossing: you can either build a raft or you can find some swimming apparatus. Here is a third way: simply jump! The leap of faith! What this implies is that faith not only gives us access to very positive states of mind, but also allows us to see things as they are in an instant. As the Buddha told Piṅgiya – his faith will allow him 'to go to the far shore'.

But doesn't this contradict something that I quoted the Buddha as saying in the introduction to this book: 'Something may be fully accepted out of faith, yet it may be empty, hollow and false; yet something else may not be fully accepted out of faith, yet it may be factual, true and unmistaken'?[15] Faith, he said there, is *not* wisdom. This is just the kind of apparent contradiction that makes us reflect! Here are my thoughts. We know that the English word faith has many different meanings: it can be an unexamined belief, a hunch, an educated guess, a feeling of optimism, a deeply considered opinion, trust in someone else's wisdom. Over the last couple of pages I have been proposing a type of faith that is different from – *more than* – any of these, and perhaps stretches the word beyond what most people would consider faith to be. Something more like wisdom. But we're considering a Buddhist term, not an English one, so the question arises: does this conception of faith match anything from the Buddhist tradition? Given what the Buddha said to Piṅgiya, and what Nāgasena said to Milinda, I think it does.

I can't remember reading any Buddhist text that explicitly states this, but I'd like to propose that, just as Buddhism recognizes different levels of wisdom, so there are different levels of faith. The first level of wisdom, you may remember, is gained through *listening*, i.e. learning from another. The corresponding level of faith is *intuition*. If we didn't intuit that there was some truth in what we were hearing, then we wouldn't bother any further with it. The second level of wisdom is *reflection*. Now we think about what we've learned, and an aspect of this is testing what we've heard against reason. As we do this our intuitive sense of rightness is backed up by reason, and the Buddha called this 'reflective acceptance'. Perhaps we can call the corresponding level of faith *reflective faith*. The third level of wisdom is reached via *contemplation*. At this level we have a direct insight into what we have previously learned and reflected on and our faith is strengthened further. In fact at this point faith *becomes* wisdom. Let's call this level of faith *experiential faith*.

Wisdom and love

What is this 'other shore'? What does faith-wisdom allow us to see? At the beginning of this chapter I mentioned a study on wisdom by two psychologists. In the chapter of the book from which I quoted that study, the authors state that wisdom is a unique state, characterized by self-transcendence, which they define as being the capacity 'to move beyond individualistic concerns to more collective or universal issues'.[16] This is a rather technical and abstract way of saying that wise people care as much about the world around them, and the beings who inhabit that world, as they do about themselves. Even more simply, it means they are unselfish. The Buddhist tradition would agree with this, and we could say that the goal of Buddhism – Awakening or Enlightenment – is simply the capacity to live completely unselfishly. There is a reason for that unselfishness. You may remember that in Chapter 2 I wrote about our sense of there being a self at the centre of our experience, and that this sense of a self is an *interpretation* of our experience, not our experience itself. Enlightened people have seen through this interpretation and so live unselfishly, not *despite* the needs, wants, aversions and fears of the self, but because *in their experience* there isn't one. Faith, or imagination, is the faculty that *intuits* that state of selflessness, and we intuit it because that is our actual experience too. That

The Art of Reflection

isn't how we *interpret* our experience, of course, but it *is* how we experience it. We could say, then, that Buddhist faith is the allowing of our experience to break through our interpretations. 'I know more than I know and I must learn it from myself.'

Returning to the practice of *Buddhānussati*, tradition tells us of a number of positive results that come about from practising it. For instance, according to the Indian commentator Buddhaghosa, anyone who regularly practises *Buddhānussati*

> . . . attains the fullness of faith, mindfulness,
> understanding and merit. . . He conquers fear and
> dread. . . He comes to feel as if he were living in the
> Master's presence. . . His mind tends towards the plane
> of the Buddhas.[17]

There is another benefit to this practice, however, which isn't mentioned in the early (Pali) texts, but which is mentioned by Zhiyi – *the* great sixth century Chinese scholar and meditator. In a series of lectures called *Great Calming and Contemplation* he said:

> In the state of dhyāna . . . when our minds and bodies
> are quiet and tranquil, then all of a sudden there comes
> into the memory a recollection of the inconceivable
> merits and purity of all the Buddhas . . . As soon as we
> are dwelling in such remembrances of the Buddha's
> transcending attainments and merits, we feel springing
> up in our dhyāna-minds the development of a spirit
> of respect for all sentient life and a feeling of fraternity
> with them; we feel unfolding powers of Samādhi
> (absorption), and a sense of joy and bliss pervades
> both body and mind that wraps us in a feeling of
> righteousness and safety. At such times we are never
> disturbed by the appearance of any bad developments
> nor evil manifestations. When we retire from our dhyāna
> practice, our body seems light and active and we feel
> so confident in the possession of good qualities, that
> we expect everyone whom we meet will respect us and
> respond to our good will.[18]

When we practise *Buddhānussati* 'we feel springing up . . . a spirit of respect for all sentient life and a feeling of fraternity with them'. I wrote above that as the Buddha lay dying, the characteristic that his closest friend Ananda remembered about him was his kindness. I wrote there that 'kindness is a form of wisdom' and I promised to explain more fully what I meant by that. I hope it is now obvious. We've seen that a unique quality of wisdom is self-transcendence: the capacity 'to move beyond individualistic concerns to more collective or universal issues'. In other words, love. To be wise is to love, and if we don't love, that means there is something we haven't yet understood. We haven't yet perceived the world as it is.

This has a great bearing on reflection. I've stated more than once in this book that reflection helps us to become wiser, but I could just as well say that it helps us to love better. The aim of reflection, and contemplation, is to help us to imagine a life in which our sense of self, and therefore a feeling of estrangement from others, dissolves. That is where reflection tends towards, and where it ultimately leads. Reflection is an act of love.

Chapter Six

....

Contemplating Reality

Nothing whatever is hidden;
From of old, all is clear as daylight.

An old pine tree preaches wisdom;
And a wild bird is crying out truth.[1]

In Chapter 5 we began to explore a kind of reflection that I called contemplation. When we hold something in our attention for a while, quietly and intently absorbed in it, not thinking about anything else, not even thinking *about* the thing we're attending to, but just keeping our mind *on* it, then we are contemplating. Now this is very difficult to do. Much of the time thoughts about other things intrude and steal our attention. This is because, as I mentioned in Chapter 5, we are divided: one part of us wants to do one thing, while other parts of us pull us away to other things. We might be trying to contemplate the Buddha, for instance, but we find ourselves planning our day or worrying about a conflict we're having with a neighbour. To contemplate effectively we have to learn how to forget everything else for the time we are contemplating. How do we do that?

The classic Buddhist way of achieving that kind of concentration is through meditation. We might practise the mindfulness of breathing, for instance, in which we pay attention to the breath. Whenever the mind wanders on to other things, we bring our attention back to the breath. We do this over and over again, hundreds, thousands of times. With practice we learn to become absorbed in the breath; other interests fall away, the breath becomes more interesting and feels more pleasurable. We might in fact find ourselves in a state in which the breath is so interesting, so enjoyable, and so absorbing, that there is nothing else we want to do, nowhere else we want to be, and nothing else we want to think about. We have entered the first *dhyāna*, which is a state of sustained, absorbed happiness and pleasure. The first *dhyāna* is characterized by five factors: initial thought, sustained thought, rapture, bliss, and one-pointedness or rapt attention. The presence of the first two factors shows us that there is still some thinking involved. We might, for instance, think: 'Oh, I'm really absorbed now, great. I wonder if this is the first *dhyāna*?' Or we might think about something unconnected with the meditation practice we're doing. However, now there is so much of us involved in the practice, we're so absorbed, so interested, *enjoying* ourselves so much, that other thoughts are experienced as peripheral and unimportant, and it is therefore easy to let go of them. It's like when you've become really involved in a game – say tennis or football – or in the story of a novel or a film, and a thought about something you have to do tomorrow enters your mind. 'Who cares?' you think, 'I'll deal with that tomorrow!' The present moment is so vivid, so engaging, so all-encompassing, that other concerns are easily forgotten.

That's the first *dhyāna*, but there's even better to come! The other *dhyānas* are intensifications of this blessed state of being. In the second *dhyāna*, thoughts disappear altogether – you don't even think about the meditation practice you're doing. It's a state of quiet, still, serene, pure happiness. In the third *dhyāna*, rapture dies away, leaving only bliss and rapt attention. That might seem disappointing – why has rapture disappeared? – but actually it's a deepening of the happiness you are feeling. At this stage, as you enter an even stiller, quieter, purer and more serene happiness, rapture now seems a little excitable, and you're quite glad when it subsides. In the fourth *dhyāna* bliss dies away and is replaced by *upekṣā* – equanimity. This is a state of profound and complete contentment, deeply satisfying, in which you want nothing other than the experience of the present moment. The whole of you is now wholly attending.

Dhyāna and contemplation

This is a very brief description of the *dhyānas*. There is quite a lot of literature available that describes them in more detail, as well as how to overcome mental states that hinder us from entering them, and how to progress from one *dhyāna* to the next. Actually there are another four, even deeper and more intense than the ones I've just briefly described, but I'm not going to go into them here. If you want to know about them, and more about the four I've just briefly described, you should read a book on meditation or, even better, devote yourself to meditation practice so that you experience them yourself.[2] What I'm interested in here is their relationship to contemplation. Most Buddhist schools recognize two different types or stages of meditation. The first is called *samatha*, which means calm – 'quietude of heart', as the Pali-English dictionary puts it. The *dhyānas* are all included within this stage. The second kind is *vipassanā*, which comes from *passanā* – 'to see' – with the emphatic prefix *vi* – 'to *really* see'. *Vipassanā* is often translated as 'insight meditation', and is what I call contemplation. How do these two kinds of meditation differ from one another? In the state of *samatha* we are attending to something very intently, with the whole of our being. When we contemplate we are attending with the same absorption and intensity, but we are also trying to understand it; we are trying to see *into* it; we are trying to look beneath its appearance to perceive its reality. When we contemplate we're not thinking about something, but neither are we *just* attending: we are attending so that we may understand.

The mathematician and philosopher George Spencer Brown puts it beautifully in his book *Laws of Form*:

> To arrive at the simplest truth . . . requires years of contemplation. Not activity. Not reasoning. Not calculating. Not busy behaviour of any kind. Not reading. Not talking. Not making an effort. Not thinking. Simply bearing in mind what it is that one needs to know.[3]

He is not writing about meditation, he is referring to what he imagines was Isaac Newton's way of trying to understand something, but he describes the experience of contemplation very well. Although he says 'not making an effort', there *is* some effort involved in contemplation, though it is very subtle. It is a kind of gentle pressure – *a* wanting to understand. In other words, faith. In Chapter 4 I said that faith could be understood as a state in which we are open to the way things really are, or more simply, open-mindedness. However, that perhaps suggests a state of passivity, in which we are willing to receive knowledge and insight if it comes to us. Faith also includes an active, searching element. It is a *desire* for understanding. Not a greedy, selfish, grasping kind of desire, though. If we're in a state of *dhyāna* then we've already achieved a high degree of wholeness and fulfilment, so we won't feel the need to grasp after anything, not even wisdom.

Now you may remember that in Chapter 5 I said that, according to the literature of the *Abhidharma*, faith is present in every skilful mental state. As the *dhyānas* are highly skilful states, faith is present in them too, which implies that the desire to understand is inherent in *dhyāna*. If this is the case, you might think that all we need to do is get into *dhyāna* and we will spontaneously begin to contemplate. However, we also need to take into account another factor – pleasure! The *dhyānas* are just so enjoyable that we may end up desiring more *dhyānic* pleasure and lose sight of our desire to understand. A conflict between Freud's pleasure principle and reality principle! Football managers often talk about the need for their players to possess the 'hunger' to win. They might have a team full of the most technically skilful players, but if they're not *hungry*, they won't win any competitions. Similarly, if we are going to *see into* anything, we must *really want* to – we need that hunger! Of course the gentle pressure we need to exert when contemplating is very different from the hunger needed to win a football match – it will be much more subtle – but gentleness and subtlety are not the same as weakness. Gentle can be strong!

How to contemplate

Once we've managed to get into *dhyāna*, how do we then contemplate? In the Pali texts the Buddha recommends that we follow a sequence. His recommendation is that we should progress through the four *dhyānas* – from the first to the fourth – and then 'return', as it were, to the first *dhyāna* to contemplate. This may seem strange. Why come back to the first? If the *dhyānas* are a progressive sequence, the fourth being a deeper and more intense experience than the first, a state of more complete wholeness, wouldn't it make more sense to contemplate from one of the deeper *dhyānas,* preferably the fourth? The answer is no, and to understand why not, we must return to those factors which are present in the first *dhyāna*, but which disappear in the second: initial thought and sustained thought. If you are going to contemplate, these need to be present. In other words, there needs to be some element of thinking. This of course contradicts the quotation from George Spencer Brown above, in which he says that contemplation is 'not thinking', and it may seem to contradict what *I* wrote in Chapter 5 about contemplation being a kind of reflection in which 'we don't have many thoughts, we don't have lots of words in our heads, we don't talk to ourselves, we don't follow a line of argument.'

So I need to explain myself. In the first *dhyāna* we don't think in the way that we normally do. Let me remind you of my description of contemplation from the first paragraph of this chapter: 'When we hold something in our attention for a while, quietly and intently absorbed in it, not thinking about anything else, not even thinking *about* the thing we're attending to, but just keeping our mind *on* it, then we are contemplating.' Perhaps we can say that when we contemplate, our thought is *still*. When we contemplate, we hold one idea, one phrase, perhaps even one word, in our mind, and we try to intuit the reality that that idea, phrase or word points to. Another way of putting this is to say that we try to look *through* the idea, phrase or word to the *experience*.

To understand this better, let's return to something I wrote in Chapter 1 about the relationship between words and experiences (page 29). I said that it was important to remember that the words we use are not the things themselves. The word 'cup', for instance, symbolizes a thing that we drink from: it is not the thing itself. I said that although this is an obvious point to make, it is one we often forget, and when we do forget it, we're no longer thinking about real things or experiences, we're thinking about concepts and words. There is more to say about this. Although the words we use are not the things themselves, there *is* a relationship between them – we could say a *meaningful* relationship! Words are not completely meaningless – they do have some kind of relationship to reality. The word 'cup', for instance, although not a cup itself, does communicate *something* to people who speak English. When you hear or read the word 'cup', you don't think of an elephant, do you? Similarly, if we take a Buddhist teaching such as impermanence, although this word is not *in itself* the reality of impermanence, it does, or can, communicate that reality. When we contemplate impermanence, we hold the word very still in our mind and dwell on it. We don't think *about* it. We focus the whole of our attention – the whole of our being – on it. That's all. Of course we already understand the meaning of the word 'impermanence'. If someone were to ask us what it means we could probably give an adequate definition or description: things that are impermanent are temporary, they change, they don't remain the same. However, we may still get upset when a cherished possession wears out or when we notice that we're looking older. So then the question arises: do we *really* understand impermanence?

'Ingathering' oneself around a topic

Of course I'm using the word 'understand' in two different ways. In the first way we understand the *meaning* – the definition – which is relatively easy to do. In the second way we understand the *reality* that the word signifies, which is much more difficult. It's difficult because to wholly understand something, the whole of us needs to be engaged; we need to be wholly present. The French philosopher Gabriel Marcel, whom we have already encountered in Chapter 2 of this book, says that 'there can be no contemplation without a kind of inward regrouping of one's resources, or a kind of ingatheredness; to contemplate is to ingather oneself in the presence of whatever is being contemplated.'[4] What a wonderful word he has coined: *ingatheredness*! We could say that the four *dhyānas* are progressively deeper experiences of ingatheredness. When we understand the word meaning of something, say impermanence, we understand with one part of ourselves: our reason. To really understand impermanence – to understand the *reality* of impermanence – we need to ingather the rest of our being around that mainly cognitive understanding.

Most people find that it's not easy to progress through the *dhyānas* in the way that the Buddha recommended. I know some people who have experienced all four 'lower' *dhyānas*, as well as one or two who have experienced the 'higher' *dhyānas*, though only on intensive meditation retreats. Even then it's not common, so it's unlikely that we'll be able to experience all four *dhyānas* while in the midst of our everyday lives. So does this mean we'll have to put off the practice of contemplation until we go on retreat? No, it doesn't, because we don't have to experience all four *dhyānas* to contemplate effectively. It's good if we can because the more ingathered we are, the more likely it is that we'll be able wholly to understand what it is that we're contemplating. However, the first *dhyāna* represents a sufficient degree of ingathering for effective contemplation, and if we meditate regularly we will find ourselves in the first *dhyāna* every now and then. In fact, you may well have experienced it outside of meditation practice. Let's recall what Ted Hughes said about fishing – how he used to sit for hours watching his float, and how 'all the little nagging impulses, that are normally distracting your mind, dissolve . . . once they have dissolved, you enter one of the orders of bliss.' Let's also remember Nazneen from the novel *Brick Lane*, who became 'whole and pure' as she sat on the floor of her living room, watching ice skating on the TV: 'The old Nazneen was sublimated and the new Nazneen was filled with white light, glory.' I think what these passages show us is that *dhyāna* is not very far away from our usual day-to-day experience. It's natural. It's what happens when we drop all of our 'hopes, random thoughts, petty anxieties and selfish wants' and relax into the present moment.

Yesterday I hosted a school visit to the Manchester Buddhist Centre. There were 16 pupils, aged 13 and 14. At one point in the visit I asked them if they'd like to try a short meditation, and they quite enthusiastically agreed. I led them in a simple awareness practice, suggesting that first they listen to sounds, then notice physical sensations in the body, and then rest their awareness on their breath. Apart from two or three who got the giggles, they all sat perfectly still and quiet. When I brought the practice to a close after five minutes, most of them kept their eyes closed and continued to meditate. I didn't say anything until they had all opened their eyes a few minutes later, and I then asked them if they'd enjoyed the experience. Nearly all of them said that they had, so I asked them what it was that they'd enjoyed. The ones who spoke told me that they'd enjoyed the experience of calm, and of having no thoughts. I then led a slightly longer meditation and they had a similar experience. Some of them wanted to do a longer meditation. None of them had meditated before and yet here they were having an experience that sounded from their descriptions like the first or second *dhyāna*. Admittedly that was unusual. Children don't often get into a meditative state so easily, but most of the children in this particular class were interested and *wanted* to meditate.

Flow

I'm sure you have had this experience, if not in meditation, then when you've been doing something that you really enjoy, such as playing a sport, reading a gripping novel, gardening, playing a musical instrument, or whatever it is that you most like doing. Something you enjoy so much that you are completely taken up with it, so that there is nothing of you left over. You lose track of time, forget all your worries and even forget yourself for a while – a state of blessed self-forgetfulness! I don't mean a loss of self-awareness, but a state in which you no longer think of yourself conceptually. That is, when you become absorbed in,

The Art of Reflection

say, reading a novel, you don't think 'I am really enjoying this novel', which suggests a divided consciousness (yourself and the novel). When you're really absorbed in it, the division between you and the novel disappears. The Hungarian psychologist Mihali Csikszentmihalyi called it the state of Flow, which comes about when your skills are equal to the task in hand. So if, for example, you're playing tennis with someone with a similar level of skill, or perhaps just a little better, then you'll experience Flow. If your opponent has a much lower level of skill than you, you'll get bored, and if they are much better than you, you'll get stressed. Either way you won't enjoy the game. But when you play someone who is about as good as you are, or perhaps just a little better, then you have to really concentrate to keep up. You become absorbed, fully taken up with the game, thoughts about other things disappear, which means the past and the future drop away, and you are living fully in the present. I find it quite easy to get into this state when I'm doing things I enjoy, such as reading, writing, thinking or listening to music. Other people I know also get into this state doing things that they enjoy: painting, cycling, singing, playing football etc. The only downside is that we can't contemplate reality when playing football or singing or whatever: our attention is fully taken up with the thing that we're doing, and there's no space left for anything else. So from the point of view of contemplation, meditation has a distinct advantage over other forms of activity.

That may be so, but what if you find that you enter the state of Flow easily when you're reading or playing table tennis – or whatever it is that you like doing – but consistently don't enter into it when you meditate? A student from one of my Buddhism courses recently told me that she found the mindfulness of breathing practice very hard: she couldn't keep her attention focused on the breath for more than a few seconds at a time. I asked her if she did become concentrated when engaged in any other activity, and after a little thought she told me that she did when she painted or read. So she didn't have a problem *concentrating*, she had a problem concentrating *on the breath*. In Chapter 3, when discussing the ability to dwell on a topic, I said that a key to paying attention is interest. If we're interested in something we'll be able to sustain our attention quite easily. That's why this student found it easy to become absorbed in painting and reading but not the mindfulness of breathing. What are we to do if we have the same problem as this student? One thing we can do is try to *become* interested in the breath (or whatever it is that we're meditating on). Things tend to become more interesting as we pay attention to them. One of the reasons we don't find the breath interesting is because we don't *know* it very well, even though we're breathing all the time! It can be taken for granted, like an old piece of furniture that's been in our house for as long as we can remember: what's interesting about that? Or like someone we've known all our lives, so that we think we already know everything about them there is to know (which is probably not true!). When we regard the breath in this way we're not really aware of it *as it is*, we're aware of it as an *idea*. We know we're breathing, but we don't know the actual felt sensations of the breath. When we start paying attention to those sensations, we may find that the breath starts to become very interesting!

In Chapter 5 I wrote about the experience of occasionally *entering into* the contemplation of the Buddha with my whole being. I likened it to driving through some countryside in a car, looking *out at* the countryside from inside the car, but then stopping and getting out of the car and walking *in* the countryside. I sometimes have a similar experience with the mindfulness of breathing. Much of the time it feels as if I am looking at the breath from outside, and this experience is not really very interesting. Sometimes, though, I seem to slip down *into* the breath. I *inhabit* it; it *envelops* me. I'm reminded of Heidegger's etymology of the word interest: 'to be among and in the midst of things, or to be at the centre of a thing and to stay with it.' When I experience the breath in this way it's no longer merely a repetitive (and therefore boring) bodily function. It is now the moving, subtle, constantly changing inflow and outflow of life: interesting, engaging, enjoyable, and fascinating.

However, there is something else we can say about interest. I have said that there are two great stages of meditation: *samatha* and *vipassanā*. The first stage has to be practised for some time before trying to practise the second stage: we need to learn to become concentrated, calm, and emotionally positive before we contemplate reality. In Gabriel Marcel's words, 'to contemplate is to ingather oneself in the presence of whatever is being contemplated.' However, he went on to say 'and this in such a fashion that the reality, confronting which one ingathers oneself, itself becomes a factor in the ingathering.'[5] In other words, whatever it is that we're contemplating helps us to become *more* concentrated. The Chinese meditation master Zhiyi taught that *samatha* and *vipassanā* needed to be balanced, like the two wheels of a chariot or the wings of a bird, and he recommended *vipassanā* to counteract problems we might encounter when trying to practise *samatha*:

> Often during the progress of the sitting the mind
> will become darkened or obscured or inattentive or
> unconscious or sleepy. On such occasions we should
> practise a reflecting insight; . . . If, as soon as we employ
> insight, we notice that the mind is more serene and pure
> as well as tranquil and peaceful, then we know that
> insight was adapted to our need and we should employ
> it at once, in order to complete the pacification.[6]

A friend of mine who has been meditating for over thirty years told me that he experiences *dhyāna* more often when contemplating than he does when doing the mindfulness of breathing. This is because he finds the object of his contemplation more compelling than he does the breath. Of course this will only be so if you're actually interested in the object of your contemplation. It has to matter to you.

Contemplating impermanence

There are many traditional objects of contemplation in the various Buddhist traditions, but for the rest of this chapter I'm going to discuss just one, on the basis that once we know how to contemplate one thing we can contemplate anything. Impermanence is one of the three *lakkhaṇa* – marks or characteristics of existence – the other two being suffering or pain, and no-self. We explored these last two characteristics a little in Chapter 2, *Learning from Experience*. I've chosen to concentrate on the contemplation of impermanence in this chapter partly because of its universal significance. No matter what kind of person we are, no matter what we believe, we're all affected by change, we're all growing older, and we're all going to die. My principal reason for choosing impermanence, though, is that it's what I contemplate most often, and whenever possible I prefer to write from my own experience. I'm now 56 years old, and I've watched my hair change from blond to brown to grey, I've watched my stomach grow large, and I've watched – with some fascination – gravity pull my face earthwards. I was once good-looking, and I used to enjoy catching a glimpse of myself in a mirror or a shop window. Now I see a rather tired-looking middle-aged man peering back – is that really me? Strange! Not that I mind very much. I'm happier now than I was when I was younger. But I'm also well aware of where this is leading. I'm over halfway through my life. I'm going to die. Of course I've always 'known' that – everyone dies – but recently I have started to really believe it, and I need to come to terms with it. It's like a puzzle that I can't get my head around – a serious puzzle. It matters to me.

Two things that are *not* impermanent

Of course I'm not the only thing that's impermanent – everything is. Well, nearly everything. The Buddha said that 'all compounded things are impermanent'. Compounded is a translation of the Pali word *saṅkhata*, which means 'made up', or 'put together'; that is, compounded things are made up of more than one thing. *Saṅkhata* also has the connotation of 'dependent' or 'conditioned'. Compounded things are impermanent *because* they depend for their existence on the things they are made of. Let's take as an example a wooden table, which is made up of a sheet of wood for the top, plus four sticks for the legs. If one of the legs falls off or breaks, then there will be effectively no table because without the broken leg it won't be able to function as a table. It will fall over. The table, to be a table, depends on each of the four legs. It also depends on the top, because without it you'd just have four sticks. Of course, when one of the legs falls off you can mend it, but one day another leg will fall off, or the top will crack, and there will come a day when the table is so patched up that you decide you may as well throw it away or burn it.

So what is uncompounded? Depending on which tradition you follow, there are just one or two uncompounded things in this universe. The one thing is Enlightenment. The two are Enlightenment and space. Enlightenment is considered to be uncompounded because it's not made up of more than one thing – it's a state of complete wholeness. And it's not dependent for its continued existence on anything else – once you're Enlightened you can never regress to unenlightenment. Of course, to *become* Enlightened depends on many conditions – we need to practise the Dharma over a long period of time – but once we're Enlightened, it doesn't depend on any other conditions for its continued existence. So Enlightenment is permanent. What about death, though? The Buddha died, didn't he? Wasn't that the end of his Enlightened state? Now we come to a Buddhist mystery. According to Buddhist tradition all beings are reborn after death except for those who are Enlightened. Enlightened beings aren't reborn, *but neither are they not reborn*. So what happens to them? Rebirth and no-rebirth are probably the only two categories we can imagine: we are either completely annihilated at death or we carry on in some way, in heaven or hell or this world or another planet or some other place. Materialists believe the first and religious people believe the second. However, the Buddha said that Enlightenment goes beyond our categories of thought. We can't imagine it. Perhaps the problem is the category of time. Perhaps Enlightenment exists outside of time? In which case I was wrong to say that Enlightenment is permanent, which is to say that it continues in time, forever. Perhaps it would be better to say that, whereas compounded things are impermanent, uncompounded things are unimaginable.

The other uncompounded thing, according to one tradition anyway, is space. Like Enlightenment, space is whole – it's not made up of more than one thing, and for that reason is also not dependent on anything for its continued existence. This may be at odds with modern scientific understandings of space – the Big Bang theory – but I'm just telling you how an ancient Indian Buddhist tradition conceived it.

Two sides to impermanence

Enlightenment and space are wonderful things to contemplate, but I'm going to return to my chosen topic, impermanence. From our (unenlightened) point of view there are two sides to impermanence – there's the aspect that we don't want and the aspect that we do. Let's start with the aspect that we don't want. You and I are impermanent. We're growing old and one day we'll die. All our friends and relations are impermanent too. Our children! What a thought! Not only that, our 'world' – the whole society we grew up in, with its language and customs, its music, literature, paintings and sculpture, its breakthroughs in science and medicine, its buildings and healthcare systems – is going to break down and cease to exist at some point in the future. And will be forgotten. One day there will come a time when no-one remembers me. Not even my name! There will come a time when no-one remembers the society in which I grew up – the music, the books, the paintings, all the accumulated knowledge and experience of so many millions of people. There will come a time when life has died out on this planet. There will come a time when this planet itself no longer exists. And there will be no-one around to remember it. Everything we know will have disappeared completely, without trace.

Wow, that's pretty depressing isn't it? Let's move on to the aspect that we do want. The traffic jam you are stuck in won't last forever, even if it feels as if it will, and the difficult day you're having will probably end with you going to bed and sleeping. The seed you planted will grow into a beautiful flower, and the raw ingredients you've put together in a pan over a flame will become a delicious meal. You can change your state of mind from grumpy to cheerful, and you can become wiser and kinder than you currently are. If it weren't for impermanence none of this would be possible. Nothing would grow, you wouldn't be able to make anything, and you wouldn't be able to change – you'd have to remain exactly as you are now, forever. And everything in your world would remain the same too. Would you want that?

All this is implicit in that simple word 'impermanence'. Not that you think about all this when you're contemplating. No, you will have already done all your thinking beforehand: you'll have thought about all the things that are impermanent, you'll have asked yourself whether there is anything at all in the universe that might be permanent (is space really permanent?), and you'll have seen all the implications and ramifications of impermanence on your life. Having done all that, the word 'impermanence' will now hold all that meaning, all that significance, without your needing to keep on thinking about it. As Kamalasila writes in his book *Meditation: the Buddhist Way of Tranquillity and Insight*:

> It is rather like gazing at a lovely jewel that has been
> laid on a piece of dark velvet cloth. We do not have
> to make any effort to see its beauty; more and more
> beauty simply reveals itself as we become more
> accustomed to looking. At this stage we do not even
> try, actively, to understand anything; we simply allow
> ourselves to be affected by the truth, by the reality of our
> contemplation.[7]

Reflecting with the whole of your body (revisited)

In Chapter 5 I said that when we contemplate we should aim to do so with all of our senses and faculties involved, including our body. I now want to say a little more about this. As you contemplate you will have certain emotional responses – sometimes you will feel inspiration, sometimes fear, sometimes sadness, sometimes joy, sometimes resistance – and these responses will be felt in your body. Recently I was contemplating the first verse of the *Jāra Sutta* (the discourse on old age) from the *Sutta-Nipāta*:

> Truly this life is short; one dies even less than one
> hundred years old. Even if anyone lives beyond (one
> hundred years), then he dies because of old age.[8]

As I contemplated this verse I began to have a sense of sadness or poignancy. It was a very delicate emotion, perhaps close to what Naomi Shihab Nye calls 'tender gravity' in her poem 'Kindness'. I felt it in my heart area and in my throat. I then asked myself why I felt sad, and I realized it was because I had wasted so much of my life in unaware states, allowing time to pass in a half-lived way. I then took my attention to this sadness, felt in my heart and throat, and I noticed that there was something else too – a sense of possibility or potentiality. It was as if the sadness I was feeling also somehow contained liberation, as if it could liberate itself into joy. I then realized that as well as feeling sad about all the time I had wasted, there was also a sense of the poignant beauty of the shortness of life – and a sense of how precious it is. The sadness then changed from a delicate pain, which had a kind of nucleus around my heart area, to a subtle opening, spreading itself out to the rest of my body as a warm pleasure, but still with a tinge of sadness.

You might also feel at times a resistance to the truth that you are contemplating. This resistance may be felt as a slight hardening of the heart or a tension in some part of your body – perhaps in your shoulders or back. This hardness and tension is you holding on to your 'self', which is being threatened by the Dharma. You can then take your attention to this hardening and tension and invite the hardness to soften, the tension to relax. You need to be patient with yourself because you can't will yourself to let go. All you can do is attend to the hardness and tension with kindness, and see if the tension will relax in its own time. If the hardness does soften and the tension does relax, then you are letting the Dharma in a little more. Don't worry or feel discouraged if you are unable to let go in the contemplation itself. If you keep contemplating the Dharma, little by little, you will let it in. You may also find that the effects of the contemplation occur later, when you are doing something else. For instance, you may find that you are a little less rigid in some of your views; or when talking to a friend you

The Art of Reflection

are a little more open to them; or when reading a Dharma text you understand it more deeply than you did before.

Impermanence is not some arcane, esoteric truth that one has to be initiated into. It's blindingly obvious – we just have to look around us to see it. The trouble is that we spend a lot of our energy trying to ignore and evade it. So when we contemplate impermanence, we aren't trying to see something subtle or elusive or abstruse; we are simply trying to stop denying what is right in front of us. As the quote I have used for the heading of this chapter states:

> Nothing whatever is hidden;
> From of old, all is clear as daylight.

As such, contemplation is a coming-to-terms with the reality that is all around and within us, rather than a trying-to-understand something obscure and difficult. So when we have a deeper insight into impermanence, it's not so much that we have learned some new information, it's more that we have accepted the obvious truth more deeply than we were previously able to.[9]

I've just used the phrase 'deeper insight', and I'd like us to be careful here. It is probably not very useful when contemplating to think in terms of gaining Insight (with a capital I). If we think in these terms we can be waiting for the Big Experience to happen and dismiss some of the real learning, the subtle shifts of perspective, that can occur. I've found it more useful to think in terms of deepening my understanding rather than gaining Insight. In traditional terms, this is the gradual, rather than the sudden approach to Enlightenment – we could say the 'incremental', rather than the 'road-to-Damascus', approach.

How to contemplate impermanence

It's best to familiarize yourself with your choice of topic before you contemplate it in meditation – study it, discuss it, think about it, question it. If you are not familiar with it or have not thought about it beforehand, when you come to contemplate it you may find that you are not yet fully convinced of its truth, and this will hinder your contemplation. For instance, when contemplating impermanence, if you are not convinced that all compounded things *are* impermanent, there will be an inner voice saying 'Hmm, not sure about this', or 'Not all of them, surely?' You need to have done your thinking and questioning beforehand, so that you are convinced that all compounded things are, in fact, impermanent. This will allow you to reflect with a minimum of discursiveness and distraction. It could be of course that you think you agree with the proposition, but when you start to meditate on it, doubts enter your mind. This is natural, and you will need to do some more studying and thinking before you return to your contemplation. This is a very useful process because you will be finding out whether you really understand, or assent to, the idea that all compounded things are impermanent.

Earlier I made the point that if we reflect on all the different things that are impermanent, when we come to contemplate it, all we will need to do is call to mind the word 'impermanence' and it will 'hold' all these specific examples. However, it's also useful at times to be very specific. In Chapter 1 I quoted the philosopher Schopenhauer, who wrote: 'Concepts always remain universal, and so do not reach down to the particular; yet it is precisely the particular that has to be dealt with in life.'[10] Impermanence is a concept. It's universal, that is to say, abstract. What we need to do is allow that abstract concept of impermanence to 'reach down to the particular' – my car, my table, my house, my body, my partner, my child. So you might sometimes take a valued object and contemplate its impermanence.

Another thing you can contemplate is the impermanence of the breath. The mindfulness of breathing is often taught and practised as a *samatha* practice, that is, as a way of calming the mind, bringing it to a point of stillness, and entering a state of absorption. However, it can also be practised as a *vipassanā* meditation. Once you have concentrated your mind on the breath you can then introduce the thought that the breath is impermanent. It's always moving, coming and going, and no two breaths are exactly alike. Like all other compounded things,

The Art of Reflection

it's in a state of flux, and, of course, one day you'll breathe out for the last time.

You can also contemplate a poem, or a part of a poem, that expresses impermanence in a way that really 'hits the spot' for you. The poem that does it for me is the Japanese monk Kukai's 'To a Nobleman in Kyoto'. Here is part of it:

You ask me why I entered the mountain deep and cold,
Awesome, surrounded by steep peaks and grotesque
    rocks,
A place that is painful to climb and difficult to descend,
Wherein reside the gods of the mountain and the spirits
    of trees.

Have you not seen, O have you not seen,
The peach and plum blossoms in the royal garden?
They must be in full bloom, pink and fragrant,
Now opening in the April showers, now falling in the
    spring gales;
Flying high and low, all over the garden the petals
    scatter.
Some sprigs may be plucked by the strolling spring
    maidens,
And the flying petals picked by the flittering spring
    orioles.

Have you not seen, O have you not seen,
The water gushing up in the divine spring of the garden?
No sooner does it arise than it flows away forever:
Thousands of shining lines flow as they come forth,
Flowing, flowing, flowing into an unfathomable abyss;
Turning, whirling again, they flow on forever,
And no one knows where they will stop.

Have you not seen, O have you not seen,
That billions have lived in China, in Japan,
None have been immortal, from time immemorial:
Ancient sage kings or tyrants, good subjects or bad,
Fair ladies and homely – who could enjoy eternal youth?

Noble men and lowly alike, without exception, die away;
They all have died, reduced to dust and ashes;
The singing halls and dancing stages have become the
    abodes of foxes.
Transient as dreams, bubbles or lightening, all are
    perpetual travellers.

Have you not seen, O have you not seen,
This has been man's fate, how can you alone live
    forever?
Thinking of this, my heart always feels torn;
You, too, are like the sun going down behind the western
    mountains,
Or a living corpse whose span of life is nearly over.[11]

I particularly like the first line of each verse: *Have you not seen,
O have you not seen?* Isn't it obvious? Are you blind? Kukai is
suggesting that the Nobleman in Kyoto is in denial!

Your object of contemplation doesn't have to be in the form
of words. It can be an image that expresses impermanence. After
all, the word 'impermanence' is just a symbol – four syllables,
or a number of lines on a page – that points to a real, living
experience, and it's the living experience that we're trying to
get at. Someone I know brings to mind a memory of a time
when she was walking on stepping-stones over a stream, and
suddenly the water flowing around a rock vividly expressed
impermanence to her. Last weekend I was in Dublin and I went
to the National Gallery. The painting that most impressed me
was *The Fisherman's Mother* by Helen Mabel Trevor. It is an
almost full-length portrait of an old woman sitting, her hands
resting on the handle of her walking stick, a rosary hanging
from her fingers. She wears a black dress with a dark blue
cloak resting on her shoulders, and a lilac head scarf. She looks
straight at the viewer, and because she is bent over a little, she
has to look up at us. She is very old, her face and hands very
wrinkled, yet there is something vibrantly alive about her. She
may be smiling – it's hard to be sure because of the angle of

The Art of Reflection

her head – but certainly her eyes are. Her inner life seems to shine through her skin, and it's beautiful. I've found a photo of the painting on flickr, and as I look at it now I feel the same tranquillity and happiness as when I first saw the picture. The painting is, for me, symbolic of two aspects of impermanence: physical decay and spiritual development. If I reach her age I'd like to look as radiant as she does.

Before actually contemplating impermanence, it is important that you do a session of *samatha* practice, perhaps especially the mettā bhāvanā, or Development of Loving Kindness (see page 48 for a brief outline of this meditation). This is important because in contemplating impermanence we are introducing reflections that inevitably include old age, death, loss etc., and you will need to try to make sure that these reflections do not tip you into a depression or a pessimistic mood. If you know that you are susceptible to depression or low moods, or that you have a tendency to look on the dark side of life, it may be best to reflect mainly on the positive aspects of impermanence, i.e. the fact that impermanence makes the spiritual life possible; that we can change for the better; that we can make spiritual progress. Concentrate on the inner radiance of *The Fisherman's Mother* rather than her wrinkled face and knotted hands!

The result of contemplating impermanence

My teacher, Sangharakshita, once said that the biggest problem of the spiritual life is to find emotional equivalents to our intellectual understanding. For most of us our intellectual understanding goes ahead, as it were, of our emotions. We can understand something with our reason without our emotions being party to that understanding. That's why we can understand, for instance, that our possessions are impermanent but get upset when one of them wears out, or breaks, or is taken away from us. The emotional equivalent to the intellectual understanding of impermanence is equanimity in the midst of change, even when change involves the loss of something. In other words, we no longer mind. Change, alteration, decay, cannot disturb our inner peace.

Tradition also tells us that the contemplation of impermanence results in an insight or liberation called the *animitta samādhi*, which means something like 'absorption in the signless'. We've seen that words are symbols, or we could say *signs*, that point, as it were, to things or experiences. Although there is some sort of relationship between words and things – a cup is not an elephant! – nevertheless, words are not the things themselves. The *animitta samādhi* is the realization that words simply cannot adequately describe the way things are. The words we use to describe our experience, even as we are having that experience ('Now I'm diving into the water'), are additional. They are not an essential part of the experience. But what is the connection between this insight and impermanence? When we name something we fix it. A name is something like a snapshot of a friend – there she is, frozen in time, as it were. We recognize her, but the snapshot is not her. There is a difference. One of the differences is that the snapshot is only two-dimensional, whereas our friend is three-dimensional. Another difference is that in the snapshot she is completely still – *frozen,* as I've put it – whereas our friend is moving all the time, even when she is being still. That is, she's breathing, her eyelids are closing and opening, blood is moving in her veins, all of which expresses vitality and life. All this is absent from the snapshot, so the snapshot is an inadequate representation of our friend – it cannot do her justice. (I'm aware that good photographers manage somehow to capture the life and movement of a person, but even the best photo is, in the end, a photo and not the person.) OK, so how about a moving film of our friend? Surely that will record our friend's movement and so will be a much more adequate record of her? That's true, but a film is similar to a snapshot in that it is a record of our friend at a particular time. Neither the snapshot nor the film shows the *impermanence* of our friend. We've all seen photos and cine- or video-films of our friends or relations taken some years previously, and we've all had the strange, and sometimes humorous, experience of recognizing them but simultaneously noticing how different they now are. They are not the same person.

So let's come back to words. When we name something – a thing or an experience – we freeze it, as it were. There is something on my desk that we call a pencil. Once I've used it a few times I

The Art of Reflection

have to sharpen the point, which I do by shaving off a part of the lead, and with that, part of the wood. So now it's not the same as it was a few minutes ago. It's smaller. Not noticeable to the naked eye, so no problem. In six months though, after many shavings, the pencil is a few inches smaller – in fact it now looks quite different. It's short and dumpy, whereas it used to be long and spindly. We still call it a pencil though. The word pencil doesn't do justice to the thing lying on my desk. You might object to this, pointing out that I've also used other words – short, dumpy, long and spindly – which surely do justice to the change my pencil has undergone. True, but these words only describe the pencil at a certain point in time – like a snapshot. Some time ago it was long and spindly, and now it's short and dumpy. In a few more weeks I will have sharpened it further, to the point where I won't be able to use it any more, and it will be just a small circle of wood with a piece of lead inside. Similarly, the name my parents gave me 56 years ago, when I was a small, babbling and incoherent baby, is still the name my family call me, even though I'm now a tall, sophisticated and articulate adult! Biologists tell us that over a seven-year period every cell in our body is renewed, which means I've become a completely different person seven times since I was first called by that name. 35 years ago I was given a Buddhist name, which goes some way to doing justice to my changing nature. Perhaps we should change our name every seven years! Admittedly this could become very confusing!

Of course, from a practical point of view, naming things and people is quite unproblematic. The word pencil manages to describe both the long spindly one as well as the short dumpy one, and when my friends say Ratnaguna, I turn around and answer them. Words *do* have a relationship to reality. However, from the spiritual point of view, words also have a problematic element to them, in that they are like snapshots that freeze things and experiences in time, and in doing so they subtly condition our perception of things. When we use the word pencil or Ratnaguna, we tend unconsciously to assume that the pencil or the person is, like the word, unmoving, fixed, and permanent. The world is ever-moving and impermanent, whereas words tend to fix things.

The *animitta samādhi* – the 'absorption in the signless' – is the direct perception of the *movingness* and impermanence of the world, and with that, the realization that words simply cannot describe how the world really is.

Reflecting on insight

And with that thought we return to something I wrote in the introduction to this book. There I discussed the Three Levels of Wisdom – listening, reflecting, and contemplating, and I mentioned the Sarvāstivāda school, which taught that reflection functions as an intermediary between the first and third levels of wisdom. You may remember that you get from the first level – 'the word' – to the third level – 'the experience' – by means of the second level – reflection. The Sarvāstivādins also say that you need to go from the experience to the word, and again, you do this by means of reflection. In the introduction I gave one reason for returning, as it were, from the experience to the word: when you have an experience that you interpret as insight, you need to check it against the teachings to make sure it's a genuine insight, and you do that by means of reflection. However, there are two more reasons.

The first is to do with communication. If you want to tell others about your experience you have to put it into words. The words will be inadequate, you won't be able to communicate it fully, but you may get something across. To borrow Schopenhauer's metaphor, you need to make a mosaic in the hope that people will then see the picture for themselves. There is a legend that the Buddha, just after his Enlightenment, feared that his experience was just too subtle, too profound, too far beyond the sphere of reason, for others to understand, and so came to the conclusion that it was not worth even trying to teach. However, Brahmā Sahampati, the King of the Gods, pleaded with him. He said that there were some 'with little dust in their eyes' who *would* understand if they were given the opportunity. As a result of Brahmā Sahampati's request, the Buddha did decide to teach. Successfully, as we know. This is a puzzling story – why did the Buddha need a god to persuade him to teach? One possible interpretation is that Brahmā Sahampati symbolizes the awakening of the Buddha's compassion. Just after his Enlightenment the Buddha was so contented, so deeply happy, that he wanted to live out the rest of his days enjoying the peace of Enlightenment, 'far from the madding crowd'. As it was likely that people wouldn't understand his teaching, why not stay at home, as it were, quietly absorbed in the experience of Enlightenment? Brahmā Sahampati symbolizes the Buddha's realization that, even if only a few people were to understand his teaching, it would be worth making the effort to teach.

However, there is another way we could interpret this episode. The Buddha's Enlightenment was, as we know, beyond the sphere of reason, so how was he to communicate it? Was it possible? Initially he thought not. Brahmā Sahampati comes along and tells him it *is* possible and he tells him why. He *reasons* with the Buddha. So we could say that he symbolizes the Buddha's reflection. He is the god of reflection! – the intermediary between the experience and the word.

The third reason for moving from the experience to the word is to enable you to communicate with yourself about your experience. This may seem a strange thing to say, but remember that insight needs to involve the whole of your being, and when you have a direct experience of reality, unmediated by concepts, then *at that time* your reasoning faculty, your thinking mind, is not involved. Therefore a part of you is left out of the experience and you now need to include it: you need to explain to yourself what happened. So you reflect on the experience and this helps you to understand its implications, and this in turn deepens the original insight. Let's say that you have a direct insight into impermanence. You may not see at the time that some aspects of your life – some of your current interests and preoccupations – are incompatible with that insight. This realization may only occur later, as you reflect on the experience. It could be, for instance, that it no longer makes sense to continue in your career, which you now realize was based on a false assumption of permanence. Or you see that your attempts to be successful or popular are ultimately futile. Or you realize that you need to treat your friends and relations much more considerately and affectionately, as you or they may not be around for very much longer.

Imagine that you have just won a very large amount of money – say twenty million pounds. You are now very rich: you can give up your job if you want to, buy a new home, a new set of clothes, and go on the holiday of a lifetime. Right now, though, you still have your old job, you are sitting in your old home (or maybe you are jumping up and down with elation!), and you are still wearing your old clothes. In fact, the money has not even gone into your bank account yet, so although you are rich, there's not much you can do with your wealth immediately. Eventually the money does reach your account, and you decide to hand your notice in to your employer, you buy a beautiful house, and some new and rather expensive clothes, and you book a holiday. You also give substantial amounts of money to some of your friends and relations who are in financially difficult circumstances, and you buy your parents a new house too. You then meet with a financial advisor, who tells you how best to invest your money. You set up some standing orders to some of your preferred charities and you even start talking to a few friends about setting up your own charity to help homeless children in Rio de Janeiro – something you have felt strongly about ever since you went on holiday there a few years ago.

When you first discovered that you'd won the twenty million pounds you hadn't yet experienced – or even seen – all the implications of suddenly becoming rich. It was only during the following few weeks and months that you began to realize those implications. Not only could you buy yourself a new home, you could also give money to some friends who really needed it. Not only could you give up your job, you could also set up a new charity, allowing you to spend your time doing something that you felt passionately about. Similarly, when you first have that insight, you are immediately freer than you were before the insight, but you haven't yet seen or experienced all the implications of that freedom. That comes with time and reflection.

Also, if you don't reflect on the insight, you risk forgetting it. My teacher, Sangharakshita, once used the metaphor of a dream to illustrate this. Sometimes you wake up and you know you have had a dream, you try to remember but you just can't get hold of it. It escapes you. He says:

> So you're not able to assimilate [the dream] into your conscious attitude. It's a bit like that with insight. It can happen that the insight is so intangible; so elusive; so subtle that you could have had it but afterwards, if you have no sort of bridge, no conceptual formulations, it's as though you just haven't had it. You can't recall it. It's gone. Just like the dream is gone.[12]

Even when we do remember a dream on waking, we can easily forget it later. If we tell ourselves about the dream though, or even better, write it down, we have a better chance of remembering it in the future. 'I went into a room, and the room was also a – what? – ahh yes, it was an aeroplane – how strange – and then . . .' Similarly it's possible to have a direct experience of impermanence. It's totally obvious to us. Now we've seen it. And the experience is so vivid, so real and true, that we think that it's changed us forever, and we'll never go back to the way we were before the experience. But we *can* forget it. We *can* revert to the way we were before the experience. People do. The significance that we saw so clearly can slip away from us unless we can find a way to remember it: a form of words that doesn't exactly describe it, but can at least jolt our memory, so that we can find a way back to the experience.

I began this book with the refrain from a song by Donovan: 'First there is a mountain then there is no mountain then there is.' You may have been puzzled by it – what did it have to do with what I wrote in the introduction? Perhaps you worked it out for yourself, but if not, here's the reason I put it there. The line is based on a Zen teaching that states that when you begin practising the spiritual life there are mountains and rivers. That is, you identify things and experiences with the words used to describe them: 'First there is a mountain'. Later, as you begin to have a deeper insight into things, you realize that words are not the things and experiences that they describe, and you go beyond reasoning, in the sense that you leave words behind: 'Then there is no mountain'. However, that is only half of the truth. Later, as your insight deepens further through reflection, you integrate this wordless, supra-rational experience into the rest of your being: 'Then there is'.

The Art of Reflection

....
Notes and references

Introduction

1 http://dictionary.reference.com/browse/art.
2 *Upāli Sutta* (*Majjhima Nikāya* 56) in *The Middle Discourses of the Buddha*, trans. Bhikkhu Ñāṇamoli and Bhikkhu Bodhi, Wisdom Publications, Boston 1995, p.481.
3 *Cankī Sutta* (*Majjhima Nikāya* 95), ibid., p.171.
4 Ibid. p.174.
5 Ibid., p.171.
6 'The *Mahāvibhāṣā* (T no. 1545, 42.217c-81.420a) and the *Abhidharmakośa* (6:143) compare the first kind of wisdom (through listening) to a swimming aid that is constantly gripped by a person who does not know how to swim. The second is like a swimming aid which the poor swimmer sometimes resorts to, sometimes not. One who possesses the wisdom from meditation (*bhāvanā mayī prajñā*) is like a strong swimmer who has crossed the river, and as such, has no more need for the support.' Piya Tan, *The Teaching Methods of the Buddha: a dynamic vision of Buddhist hermeneutics*, National University of Singapore Buddhist Society Dharma Leadership Training Course 2002, p.33, available on the internet at www.pali.house.googlepages.com/TeachingMethodsoftheBuddha.pdf.
7 There are two contemporary books that I know of that teach how to reflect: Gregory Kramer, *Insight Dialogue: The Interpersonal Path to Freedom*, Shambhala Publications, Boston 2007; and Andy Karr, *Contemplating Reality: A Practitioner's Guide to the View in Indo-Tibetan Buddhism*, Shambhala Publications, Boston 2007. The first describes a very specific way of reflecting, in dialogue with others. The second is about the third level of wisdom – contemplation – specifically, as the title suggests, as practised within the Tibetan traditions. There may be more that I'm not aware of.
8 http://dictionary.reference.com/browse/ponder?&qsrc=.

9 Rainer Maria Rilke, *Letters to a Young Poet*, trans. Stephen Mitchell, Vintage Books, New York 1986, pp.34–35.

10 *Shōbōgenzō zuimonki*, trans. Reihō Masunaga, East-West Center Press, Honolulu 1971, p.39.

Chapter One: A Reflective Life

1 Nick Hornby, *A Long Way Down*, Penguin, London 2006, p.224.

2 *Dvedhavitakka Sutta* (*Majjhima Nikāya* 19), trans. Bhikkhu Ñāṇamoli and Bhikkhu Bodhi, Wisdom Publications, Boston 1995.

3 *Dhammapada* 121–122, trans. Sangharakshita, Windhorse Publications, Birmingham 2001, pp.48–49.

4 Some people I know tell me that they don't think in words – they think in shapes and colours or in some other wordless way. I find this very hard to understand and even, I admit, believe. Perhaps this is just a lack of imagination on my part.

5 Arthur Schopenhauer, *The World as Will and Representation*, ii. 74.

6 Ibid, i. 57. Both quoted in Bryan Magee, *The Philosophy of Schopenhauer*, Oxford University Press, Oxford 1983, p.42.

7 This sequence comes from the *Madhupindika Sutta* (*Majjhima Nikāya* 18). It was taught by one of the Buddha's disciples – Maha Kaccāna – and was later endorsed by the Buddha himself. There are other, slightly different, sequences to this one, but they all make the same point.

8 This is a Buddhist adaptation of a diagram by the psychologist Mark Williams, which he used in a Powerpoint presentation called 'Mindfulness, Depression and Modes of Mind'. With thanks.

9 Alexander McCall Smith, *Friends, Lovers, Chocolate*, First Anchor Books Edition, New York 2006, p.52.

10 One in six of workers surveyed in the UK now work over 60 hours a week compared to just one in eight in 2000. Source: Dept. of Trade and Industry and Management Today survey. Britain's full-time workers put in the longest hours in Europe at 43.6 hours per week compared with the EU average of 40.3 hours per week. The number of people working over 48 hours has more than doubled since 1998, from 10% to 26%. And one in six of all workers is doing more than 60 hours. Source: Madeleine Bunting, 'Willing Slaves: How the Overwork Culture is Ruling Our Lives'.

11 35% of employees consider technology the reason for their longer working hours according to a study conducted by Kelly Global Workforce Index, which obtained the views of approximately 100,000 people in 34 countries covering North America, Europe, and Asia Pacific. http://easypr.marketwire.com/easyir/msc2.do?easyirid=95BBA2C450798961 – accessed on 16 December 2009.

12 From the *Kadamthorbu*, or *Precepts Gathered from Here and There*. Quoted in Geshe Wangyal, *The Door of Liberation*, Maurice Girodias Associates, New York 1973, p.126.

13 *Kosambiya* Sutta 48.12, *Majjhima Nikāya*.

14 From Walter Murdoch, *72 Essays*, p.16. Out of print, but available to read online on http://books.google.co.uk.

15 People who are susceptible to depression also have to watch out for this tendency, called 'rumination'. This is the tendency, when in a low mood, to think about and try to work out why we are unhappy. 'Ruminating' in this way tends to keep us in the low mood, rather than help us out of it. (See Segal, Williams and Teasdale, *Mindfulness-based Cognitive Therapy for Depression*, Guilford Press, New York 2002, pp.33–37. In traditional Buddhist terms this is an aspect of *papañca* – obsession.

Chapter Two: Learning from Experience

1 http://thinkexist.com/quotation/what_is_the_good_of_experience_if_you_do_not/344014.html

2 Martin Heidegger, *Discourse on Thinking*.

3 Alexander McCall Smith, *The Right Attitude to Rain*, Abacus, London 2007, p.73.

4 Alexander McCall Smith, *Friends, Lovers, Chocolate*, First Anchor Books Edition, New York 2006, p.215.

5 From the Gifford Lectures series, *The Mystery of Being: Reflection and Mystery 1948–1950*, Chapter V, 'Primary and Secondary Reflection: The Existential Fulcrum', Harvill Press, London 1950, pp.77–80. Also available online at http://www.giffordlectures.orgBrowse.aspPubID=TPMYSB&Volume=0&Issue=0&ArticleID=5

6 Bruner, Jerome and Postman, Leo, 'Emotional selectivity in perception and reaction', *Journal of Personality*, vol.16 (1947), pp. 69–77.

7 Quoted in a lecture called *The Meaning of Spiritual Community* by Sangharakshita, transcribed and published in Sangharakshita, *Human Enlightenment*, Windhorse Publications, London 1980, pp.59–60.

8 Walt Whitman, *Song of Myself*, verse 51.

9 For instance, see A. G. Greenwauld, 'The Totalitarian Ego: Fabrication and Revision of Personal History', *American Psychologist* 35, (1980): 603–13; M.D. Alicke et al., 'The Person Who Outperforms Me is a Genius: Maintaining Perceived Competence in Upward Social Comparison,' *Journal of Personality and Social Psychology* 72 (1977): 781–89. These and others are quoted in Mark Leary, *The Curse of the Self*, Oxford University Press, Oxford 2004.

10 Mark Leary, *The Curse of the Self*, Oxford University Press, Oxford 2004, p.12.
11 *Sutta Nipāta* 938, trans. K. R. Norman, *The Rhinoceros Horn*, Pali Text Society 1996, p.154.
12 Alloy, I. B., and Abramson, I. Y., Judgement of contingency in depressed and non-depressed students: Sadder but Wiser. *Journal of Experimental Psychology: General, 108*, 1979, pp.441–485.
13 'Compounded' is a technical term, which refers to the fact that almost everything we experience is made up – compounded – of a number of factors. For more on this, see Chapter 6, page 130.
14 Kahneman, D. and Tversky, A. (eds)., *Choices, Values and Frames*, Cambridge University Press 2000, p.58. Also Stutzer, A. 2003. 'The role of income aspirations in individual happiness', *Journal of Economic Behaviour and Organization*, 54, pp. 89–109.
15 Naomi Shihab Nye, 'Kindness', from *Words Under the Words*, Eighth Mountain Press, Portland 1998.

Chapter Three: Dwelling on a Topic

1 Franz Kafka, from *Betrachtungen über Sünde, Leid, Hoffnung und den wahren Weg* (translated as *Reflections on Sin, Suffering, Hope and the True Way*), published after Kafka's death in *Beim Bau der chinesischen Mauer* (translated as *The Great Wall of China: Stories and Reflections*). It is found at the end of Kafka's last aphorism, number 109.
2 Martin Heidegger, *Was Heißt Denken?*, translated by J. Glenn Gray as *What is Called Thinking*, Harper Perennial, New York 1968, book 1, p.5.
3 Pierre Hadot, *Philosophy as a Way of Life*, Blackwell, Oxford 1995, p.91.
4 Ibid., p. 91.
5 Francis Bacon, *Of Studies*.
6 Mark Tredinnick, *Writing Well*, Cambridge University Press. 2008, p.201.
7 Jean-Jacques Rousseau, *The Confessions*.
8 If you're interested in following up this idea, there is a whole book on the practice of reflecting with others: Gregory Kramer, *Insight Dialogue: The Interpersonal Path to Freedom*, Shambhala Publications, Boston 2007.
9 Ted Hughes, *Poetry in the Making*, Faber and Faber, London 1967, p.56.
10 Ibid., pp.57–8.
11 Marilynne Robinson, *Gilead*, Virago, London 2004, pp.204–5.
12 Ibid., pp.217–8.

Chapter Four: Reading Reflectively

1 Harold Bloom, *How to Read and Why*, Fourth Estate, London 2001, p.19.
2 Peter Ackroyd, *The Plato Papers*, Chatto & Windus, London, 1999, pp. 113–14.
3 Pierre Hadot, *Philosophy as a Way of Life*, op.cit., p.109. Here 'ruminate' is a translation of a French word – I don't know which one – but Hadot obviously doesn't mean ruminate in the sense in which it is used in modern psychology (see note 15 in Chapter 1).
4 http://en.wikipedia.org/wiki/Speed_reading
5 Friedrich Nietzsche, *Daybreak*, trans. R.J. Hollingdale, Cambridge University Press, 1982, p.5.
6 Paul Gilbert, *The Compassionate Mind*, Constable & Robinson, London 2009, p.198.
7 Ibid., p.202.
8 Hui Yung, *Translating Holy Books* (Chinese, 4th to 5th century), trans. J. P. Seaton in *The Poetry of Zen*, Shambhala Publications, Boston 2007.
9 Incidentally, you can find a very good article on reading Pali suttas on this website, called *Befriending the Suttas: Tips on Reading the Pali Discourses*, by John Bullitt. http://www.accesstoinsight.org/lib/authors/bullitt/befriending.html.
10 Richard Holloway, *Doubts and Loves*, Canongate Books, Edinburgh 2005.
11 There are a number of books available that offer commentaries on traditional Buddhist texts. To mention just a few commentaries on parts of the Pali canon: *Come and See for Yourself* by Ayya Khema – every chapter of this book is a commentary on a different short passage from the Pali Canon; *Breath By Breath*, by Larry Rosenberg, is a commentary on the Anapanasati Sutta; *Living with Awareness* by Sangharakshita, and *Satipatthana: the Direct Path to Realization* by Analayo, are both commentaries on the Satipatthana Sutta; and *Living with Kindness* by Sangharakshita is a commentary on the Metta Sutta. There are also some very good websites that have commentaries such as www.accesstoinsight.org and www. freebuddhistaudio.com.
12 *Ratnagunasamcayagatha – Verses on the Accumulation of Precious Qualities*, trans. E. Conze, Four Seasons, San Francisco 1973, p.9.
13 From Monier Monier-Williams, *A Sanskrit English Dictionary*, Motilal Banarsidass, Delhi 1995, pp.696–697.
14 *Dhammapada*, trans. Sangharakshita, Windhorse Publications, Birmingham 2001, p.13.
15 *Dhammapada*, trans. Thomas Byrom, Shambhala, Boston 1993, pp.1–2.

16 *Dhammapada*, Thanissaro Bhikkhu, Dhamma Dana Publications, Barre 1998, p.1.

17 Ibid., p.137.

18 http://changingminds.org/explanations/identity/jung_archetypes.htm.

19 *Kalāma Sutta: The Buddha's Charter of Free Inquiry*, trans. Soma Thera, Buddhist Publication Society, Kandy 1981.

20 Quoted by Hadot, ibid., p.109.

21 Along with the *Rhinoceros Sutta* from the first chapter. Not everyone is convinced that these texts are in fact earlier than other parts of the canon – see, for instance, Thanissaro's comments in the *Atthaka Vagga* (the Octet Chapter): an Introduction, on www.accesstoinsight.org.

22 Sangharakshita, *Wisdom Beyond Words*, Windhorse Publications, Birmingham 2001, p.154.

23 Hadot, ibid., p.108.

Chapter Five: Imagining the Buddha

1 *Dvedhāvitakka Sutta* (*Majjhima Nikāya* 19), trans. Bhikkhu Ñāṇamoli and Bhikkhu Bodhi, Wisdom Publications, Boston 1995.

2 Clayton, V., and Birren, J. E., *The development of wisdom across the life span: a re-examination of an ancient topic*, quoted in *Wisdom: its nature, origins and development*, ed. Robert J. Sternberg, ch.8, *The study of wise persons: integrating a personality perspective*, Lucinda Orwoll and Marion Perlmutter, Cambridge University Press, Cambridge 1990, p.168.

3 Pierre Hadot, *What is Ancient Philosophy?*, Belknap Harvard 2004, p.224.

4 Paul Gilbert, *The Compassionate Mind*, Constable & Robinson, London 2009, p.252.

5 Thanissaro's translation.

6 *Sutta-Nipāta*, Curzon Press, London 1985, pp.100–101. If you'd like to follow this up and read other translations, with notes, I recommend Bhikkhu Thanissaro's, which can be found on his website http://www.accesstoinsight.org/tipitaka/kn/snp/snp.4.10.than.html, and K.R. Norman's, in his book *The Rhinoceros Horn*, Pali Text Society, Oxford 1996, p.142.

7 All definitions from *The Oxford Universal Dictionary*, 1965.

8 From the Sanskrit version of the sūtra, translated by Luis O. Gomez in *The Land of Bliss*, University of Hawaii Press 1996, p.18.

9 Published in Sangharakshita, *The Priceless Jewel*, Windhorse Publications, Glasgow 1993, p.57.

10 Monica Ali, *Brick Lane*, Black Swan, London 2004, p.41.

11 Paravahera Vajiranana Mahāthera, *Buddhist Meditation in Theory and Practice*, Gunasena, Colombo 1962.
12 Trans. K. R. Norman, ibid., p.184.
13 *The Questions of King Milinda*, trans. T. W. Rhys Davids, vol. XXXV of *The Sacred Books of the East*, ed. Max Muller. Oxford University Press, Oxford 1890, book 2, chapter 1. p.54.
14 Ibid. p.56.
15 *Cankī Sutta* (*Majjhima Nikāya* 95), ibid., p.171.
16 Lucinda Orwoll and Marion Perlmutter, *The study of wise persons: integrating a personality perspective*, quoted in *Wisdom: its nature, origins and development*, ed. Robert J. Sternberg, Cambridge University Press, Cambridge 1990, ch. 8., p.162.
17 *Visuddhimagga – The Path of Purification*, trans. Bhikkhu Ñāṇamoli, Buddhist Publication Society 1991, p.230.
18 *A Buddhist Bible*, ed. Dwight Goddard, Beacon Press, Boston 1970, p.480.

Chapter Six: Contemplating Reality

1 From the *Zenrinkushu*, compiled by Eicho (1429–1504).
2 Two books that come to mind are: Kamalasila, *Meditation: The Buddhist Way of Tranquillity and Insight*, Windhorse Publications, Birmingham 2003; and Ajahn Brahm, *Mindfulness, Bliss and Beyond: A Meditator's Handbook*, Wisdom Publications, Boston 2006.
3 Quoted in Guy Claxton, *Hare Brain, Tortoise Mind*, Fourth Estate, London 1977, p.58.
4 Gabriel Marcel, *Reflection and Mystery*, Harvill Press, London 1950, chapter VII, 'Being in a Situation', p.126.
5 Ibid.
6 *A Buddhist Bible*, ed. Dwight Goddard, Beacon Press, Boston 1970, p.466.
7 Kamalasila, *Meditation: The Buddhist Way of Tranquillity and Insight*, Windhorse Publications, Birmingham 2003. pp.89–90.
8 *Sutta Nipāta* 4.6, from the *Atthaka Vagga*, trans. K. R. Norman, Pali Text Society, Oxford1984, p.136.
9 A friend recently pointed out to me that Pema Chödrön has suggested that the third root poison (delusion or ignorance) could be translated as denial. In fact the word 'ignorance' implies this – ignore–ance.
10 Arthur Schopenhauer, *The World as Will and Representation*, ii. 74.
11 Quoted in *Readings from the Refuge Tree of the Western Buddhist Order*, compiled and edited by Lokabandhu, privately published, no date.
12 Unedited seminar transcript, *Questions and Answers on the Mitrata Omnibus* (Tuscany Ordination Retreat 1981), section 2, p.33.

Glossary of Buddhist Terms

I have sometimes used Pali or Sanskrit words in this book – both ancient Indian languages. There is no reason why I have chosen one rather than the other in any particular case, apart from personal preference. Every time I introduce such a word I have defined it. However, words I have used more than once appear in the following glossary.

Abhidharma (Skt): the so-called 'higher teachings' of Buddhism. Sometimes said to contain the 'psychology' of Buddhism.

Anussati (Pali): Recollection or remembrance, calling to mind, keeping in mind.

Buddha (Pali and Skt): The Awakened or Enlightened One. Siddhartha Gautama, who gained Enlightenment roughly 2,500 years ago in India.

Buddhānussati (Pali): Recollection of the Buddha.

Dharma (Skt): The Truth, or the way things are. The teachings of the Buddha.

Dhyāna (Skt): a meditative state of still, calm absorption. There are said to be four 'lower' *dhyānas* and another four 'higher' *dhyānas*.

Enlightenment: The state of wisdom, the complete absence of greed, hatred and delusion.

Pali Canon: A set of Buddhist texts in the Pali language. Doctrinal basis of the Theravāda school of Buddhism.

Papañca (Pali): Mental proliferation. The mind carried away with conceptualization.

Prasāda (Skt): Faith, clearness, brightness, pellucidity, purity, calmness, tranquillity, absence of excitement, serenity of disposition, good humour, aid, mediation.

Samatha (Pali): State of calm, still absorption. 'Quietude of mind'. Includes the states of *dhyāna*.

Sangha (Pali): Followers of the Buddha who have themselves gained a high degree of wisdom.

Sutta (Pali): Discourse of the Buddha (*sūtra* in Sanskrit).

Sarvāstivāda (Skt): An ancient Indian school of Buddhism. Followers of this school are called *Sarvāstivādins*.

The Three Levels of Wisdom: *suta-maya-paññā* – wisdom through hearing; *cinta-maya-paññā* – wisdom through thinking; and *bhāvanā-maya-paññā* – wisdom through meditating (Pali).

Vipassanā (Pali): Insight.

Vitakka-vicāra (Pali): Initial thought and sustained thought. *Vitakka* is the mind first alighting on a subject, *vicāra* is the continued attention of the mind on that subject. Together they may be thought of as constituting concentrated and directed thinking.

Index

WINDHORSE PUBLICATIONS

Windhorse Publications is a Buddhist charitable company based in the UK. We place great emphasis on producing books of high quality that are accessible and relevant to those interested in Buddhism at whatever level. We are the main publisher of the works of Sangharakshita, the founder of the Triratna Buddhist Order and Community. Our books draw on the whole range of the Buddhist tradition, including translations of traditional texts, commentaries, books that make links with contemporary culture and ways of life, biographies of Buddhists, and works on meditation.

As a not-for-profit enterprise, we ensure that all surplus income is invested in new books and improved production methods, to better communicate Buddhism in the 21st century. We welcome donations to help us continue our work – to find out more, go to www.windhorsepublications.com.

The Windhorse is a mythical animal that flies over the earth carrying on its back three precious jewels, bringing these invaluable gifts to all humanity: the Buddha (the 'awakened one'), his teaching, and the community of all his followers.

Windhorse Publications	Perseus Distribution	Windhorse Books
169 Mill Road	210 American Drive	PO Box 574
Cambridge	Jackson TN 38301	Newtown NSW 2042
CB1 3AN	USA	Australia
UK		

info@windhorsepublications.com

THE TRIRATNA BUDDHIST COMMUNITY

Windhorse Publications is a part of the Triratna Buddhist Community, an international movement with centres in Europe, India, North and South America and Australasia. At these centres, members of the Triratna Buddhist Order offer classes in meditation and Buddhism. Activities of the Triratna Community also include retreat centres, residential spiritual communities, ethical Right Livelihood businesses, and the Karuna Trust, a UK fundraising charity that supports social welfare projects in the slums and villages of India.

Through these and other activities, Triratna is developing a unique approach to Buddhism, not simply as a philosophy and a set of techniques, but as a creatively directed way of life for all people living in the conditions of the modern world.

If you would like more information about Triratna please visit www.thebuddhistcentre.com or write to:

London Buddhist Centre	Aryaloka	Sydney Buddhist Centre
51 Roman Road	14 Heartwood Circle	24 Enmore Road
London E2 0HU	Newmarket NH 03857	Sydney NSW 2042
UK	USA	Australia

Also from Windhorse Publications

Satipaṭṭhāna
The Direct Path to Realization
by Anālayo

This best-selling book offers a unique and detailed textual study of the Satipaṭṭhāna Sutta, a foundational Buddhist discourse on meditation practice.

This book should prove to be of value both to scholars of Early Buddhism and to serious meditators alike. – Bhikkhu Bodhi

a gem ... I learned a lot from this wonderful book and highly recommend it. – Joseph Goldstein

An indispensible guide ... surely destined to become the classic commentary on the Satipaṭṭhāna. – Christopher Titmuss

Very impressive and useful, with its blend of strong scholarship and attunement to practice issues. – Prof. Peter Harvey, author of *An Introduction to Buddhist Ethics*

ISBN 9781 899579 54 9
£15.99 / $24.95 / €19.95
336 pages

A Guide to the Buddhist Path
by Sangharakshita

In this approachable handbook, Sangharakshita maps out the complex tradition of Buddhism. In part one he presents the theory of the religion in sections devoted to the Buddha, the Dharma and the Sangha, while in part two he explores what it means to really lead a Buddhist life and the practicalities involved.

For those wishing to deepen their knowledge and experience of Buddhism, this is a complete map of the Buddhist path.

ISBN 9781 907314 05 6
£16.99 / $23.95 / €19.95
264 pages